Porsc

MW01285577

Type 964: 1989▶1994

Technical Data
Carrera 2, Carrera 4, RS America
Turbo 3.3, Turbo 3.6

B | www.
BentleyPublishers
.com

BENTLEY PUBLISHERS™ | Automotive Reference™

Bentley Publishers, a division of Robert Bentley, Inc.
1734 Massachusetts Avenue
Cambridge, MA 02138 USA   Information that makes
800-423-4595 / 617-547-4170   the difference®

BentleyPublishers
.com

Technical contact information

We welcome your feedback. Please submit corrections and additions to our Porsche technical discussion forum at:

http://www.BentleyPublishers.com

Errata information

We will evaluate submissions and post appropriate editorial changes online as text errata or tech discussion. Appropriate errata will be incorporated with the book text in future printings. Read errata information for this book before beginning work on your vehicle. See the following web address for additional information:

http://www.BentleyPublishers.com/errata/

WARNING—Important Safety Notice

Do not use this book unless you are familiar with automotive repair procedures and safe workshop practices. This technical data book is not a substitute for full and up-to-date service information from the vehicle manufacturer or for proper training as an automotive technician. Note that it is not possible for us to anticipate all of the ways or conditions under which vehicles may be serviced or to provide cautions as to all of the possible hazards that may result.

We have endeavored to ensure the accuracy of the information in this book. Please note, however, that considering the vast quantity and the complexity of the service information involved, we cannot warrant the accuracy or completeness of the information contained in this manual.

FOR THESE REASONS, NEITHER THE PUBLISHER NOR THE AUTHOR MAKES ANY WARRANTIES, EXPRESS OR IMPLIED, THAT THE INFORMATION IN THIS BOOK IS FREE OF ERRORS OR OMISSIONS, AND WE EXPRESSLY DISCLAIM THE IMPLIED WARRANTIES OF MERCHANTABILITY AND OF FITNESS FOR A PARTICULAR PURPOSE, EVEN IF THE PUBLISHER OR AUTHOR HAVE BEEN ADVISED OF A PARTICULAR PURPOSE, AND EVEN IF A PARTICULAR PURPOSE IS INDICATED IN THE BOOK. THE PUBLISHER AND AUTHOR ALSO DISCLAIM ALL LIABILITY FOR DIRECT, INDIRECT, INCIDENTAL OR CONSEQUENTIAL DAMAGES THAT RESULT FROM ANY USE OF THE EXAMPLES, INSTRUCTIONS OR OTHER INFORMATION IN THIS BOOK. IN NO EVENT SHALL OUR LIABILITY WHETHER IN TORT, CONTRACT OR OTHERWISE EXCEED THE COST OF THIS BOOK.

Your common sense and good judgment are crucial to safe and successful service work. Think about whether the condition of your car, your level of mechanical skill, or your level of reading comprehension might result in or contribute in some way to an occurrence which might cause you injury, damage your car, or result in an unsafe repair. If you have doubts for these or other reasons about your ability to perform safe repair work on your car, have the work done at an authorized Porsche dealer or other qualified shop.

Before attempting any work on your Porsche, read **00 Warnings and Cautions** and any **WARNING** or **CAUTION** given in the book. Review the **WARNINGS** and **CAUTIONS** each time you prepare to work on your Porsche.

Part numbers listed in this manual are for identification purposes only, not for ordering. Always check with your authorized Porsche dealer to verify part numbers and availability before beginning service work that may require new parts.

Special tools are required to perform certain service operations and are recommended for use. Use of tools other than those recommended in this manual may be detrimental to the car's safe operation as well as the safety of the person servicing the car.

The vehicle manufacturer will continue to issue service information updates and parts retrofits after the editorial closing of this book. Some of these updates and retrofits will apply to specifications in this book. We regret that we cannot supply updates to purchasers of this book.

This book is published by Bentley Publishers. Porsche has not reviewed and does not vouch for the accuracy of the technical specifications and information contained in this book.

Library of Congress Cataloging-in-Publication Data

Porsche Carrera (964) 1989-1994 : technical data : Carrera 2, Carrera 4, RS America, Turbo 3.3, Turbo 3.6
    p. cm.
  Includes index.
  ISBN 978-8376-0292-9 (pbk.)
  1. Porsche automobiles--Maintenance and repair--Handbooks, manuals, etc.

TL215.P75 P647 2002
629.28'722--dc21

            2002025400

ISBN 978-0-8376-0292-9　　　**Bentley Stock No. PC94**　　　Mfg. code: PC94-03-0808, editorial closing 04 / 2002.

The paper used in this publication is acid free and meets the requirements of the National Standard for Information Sciences—Permanence of Paper for Printed Library Materials.

Manufactured in the United States of America.

0 General

00 Warnings and Cautions	**02** General
01 Vehicle Identification and VIN Decoder	**03** Maintenance

1 Engine

10 Engine Crankcase	**15** Cylinder Heads, Camshafts, Timing Chains
13 Crankshaft	**17** Lubrication System

2 Engine Management

20 Fuel Supply	**26** Exhaust System
21 Turbocharger	**27** Alternator, Battery, Starter
24 DME Fuel Injection	**28** Ignition System
25 CIS Fuel Injection	

3 Drivetrain

30 Clutch Assembly	**34** Manual Transmission (All Wheel Drive)
32 Manual Transmission (Rear Wheel Drive)	**37** Automatic Transmission
	39 Front final Drive

4 Chassis

40 Front Suspension	**46** Brakes System
42 Rear Suspension	**48** Steering
44 Alignment, Wheels, Tires	

8 Heating and A/C

87 Air Conditioning

9 Electrical

90 Electrical System

Foreword

This book covers technical data for the 1989 through 1994 Porsche 964 automobile and is specifically designed to cover only those models built for sale in the United States. This book is not a service manual and should be used solely as a reference in conjunction with factory repair and service information.

Disclaimer

We have endeavored to ensure the accuracy of the information in this book. When the vast array of data presented in the book is taken into account, however, no claim to infallibility can be made. We therefore cannot be responsible for the result of any errors that may have crept into the text. Please read **WARNING–Important Safety Notice** on the copyright page and **00 Warnings and Cautions** and the warnings and cautions that accompany the text prior to any service or maintenance work.

Bentley Publishers encourages comments from the readers of this manual with regard to errors, and suggestions for improvement of our product. These communications have been and will be carefully considered in the preparation of this and other manuals. If you identify inconsistencies in the manual, you may have found an error. Please contact the publisher and we will endeavor to post applicable corrections on our website. Posted corrections (errata) should be reviewed before beginning work. Please see the following web address:

$$\texttt{http://www.BentleyPublishers.com/errata/}$$

Porsche continues to issue service information and parts retrofits after the editorial closing of this manual. Some of this updated information may apply to procedures and specifications in this manual. For the latest information, please see the following web address:

$$\texttt{http://techinfo.porsche.com/}$$

Porsche offers extensive warranties, especially on components of the fuel delivery and emission control systems. Therefore, before deciding to repair a Porsche that may be covered wholly or in part by any warranties issued by Porsche of America, Inc., consult your authorized Porsche dealer. You may find that the dealer can make the repair either free or at minimum cost. Regardless of its age, or whether it is under warranty, your Porsche is an easy car to get serviced. So if at any time a repair is needed that you feel is too difficult to do yourself, a trained Porsche technician is ready to do the job for you.

Bentley Publishers

00 Warnings and Cautions

Please read these warnings and cautions.

WARNINGS and CAUTIONS—

See also **WARNINGS and CAUTIONS** on next page.

- Read the important safety notice on the copyright page at the beginning of the book.

- Thoroughly read each **WARNING** and **CAUTION** that accompany the text. Also review any posted corrections at www.BentleyPublishers.com/errata/ before beginning work.

- This handbook contains technical data for the Porsche 964 automobile. This handbook is not a substitute for up-to-date repair and service information from the manufacturer. Do not carry out vehicle repairs using this handbook as the source of repair or service information.

- If any procedure, tightening torque, wear limit, specification or data presented in this manual does not appear to be appropriate for a specific application, contact the publisher or the vehicle manufacturer for clarification before using the information in question.

- The use of aftermarket parts and equipment for Porsche cars, although widespread, may cause safety defects or reliability problems. Aftermarket parts may not fit or function correctly. When installing replacement parts or performing upgrades to your car, it is highly recommended that original Porsche parts be used.

- If you lack the skills, tools and equipment, or a suitable workshop, we suggest you leave vehicle repairs to an authorized Porsche dealer or other qualified shop.

- Gasoline is highly flammable. When working with fuel lines do not smoke or work near heaters or other fire hazards. Keep a fire extinguisher handy. Before disconnecting fuel hoses, wrap a cloth around fuel hoses to absorb any leaking fuel. Catch and dispose of escaped fuel. Plug all open fuel lines.

- Do not reuse any fasteners that are worn or deformed in normal use. Many fasteners are designed to be used only once and become unreliable and may fail when used a second time. This includes, but is not limited to, nuts, bolts, washers, self-locking nuts or bolts, circlips and cotter pins. Replace these fasteners with new parts.

- Do not work under a lifted car unless it is solidly supported on stands designed for the purpose. Do not support a car on cinder blocks, hollow tiles or other props that may crumble under continuous load. Do not work under a car that is supported solely by a jack. Do not work under the car while the engine is running.

- If you are going to work under a car on the ground, make sure that the ground is level. Block the wheels to keep the car from rolling. Disconnect the battery negative (–) terminal (ground strap) to prevent others from starting the car while you are under it.

- Do not run the engine unless the work area is well ventilated. Carbon monoxide kills.

- Remove finger rings, bracelets and other jewelry so that they cannot cause electrical shorts, get caught in running machinery or be crushed by heavy parts.

- Tie long hair behind your head. Do not wear a necktie, a scarf, loose clothing, or a necklace when you work near machine tools or running engines. If your hair, clothing, or jewelry were to get caught in the machinery, severe injury could result.

- Do not attempt to work on your car if you do not feel well. You increase the danger of injury to yourself and others if you are tired, upset or have taken medication or any other substance that may keep you from being fully alert.

- Illuminate your work area adequately but safely. Use a portable safety light for working inside or under the car. Make sure the bulb is enclosed by a wire cage. The hot filament of an accidentally broken bulb can ignite spilled fuel, vapors or oil.

- Catch draining fuel, oil or brake fluid in suitable containers. Do not use food or beverage containers that might mislead someone into drinking from them. Store flammable fluids away from fire hazards. Wipe up spills at once but do not store the oily rags, which can ignite and burn spontaneously.

- Observe good workshop practices. Wear goggles when you operate machine tools or work with battery acid. Wear gloves or other protective clothing whenever the job requires working with harmful substances.

- Greases, lubricants and other automotive chemicals contain toxic substances, many of which are absorbed directly through the skin. Read the manufacturer's instructions and warnings carefully. Use hand and eye protection. Avoid direct skin contact.

- Disconnect the battery negative (–) terminal (ground strap) whenever you work on the fuel system or the electrical system. Do not smoke or work near heaters or other fire hazards. Keep an approved fire extinguisher handy.

- Friction components (such as brake pads or shoes or clutch discs) contain asbestos fibers or other friction materials. Do not create dust by grinding, sanding, or by cleaning with compressed air. Avoid breathing dust. Breathing any friction material dust can lead to serious diseases and may result in death.

- Batteries give off explosive hydrogen gas during charging. Keep sparks, lighted matches and open flame away from the top of the battery. If hydrogen gas escaping from the cap vents is ignited, it will ignite gas trapped in the cells and cause the battery to explode.

- Battery acid (electrolyte) can cause severe skin burns. Flush contact area with water and seek medical attention.

- Do not quick-charge the battery (for boost starting) for longer than one minute. Wait at least one minute before boosting the battery a second time.

- Connect and disconnect a battery charger only with the battery charger switched OFF.

- Connect and disconnect battery cables, jumper cables or a battery charger only with the ignition switched OFF. Do not disconnect the battery while the engine is running.

- Do not allow the battery charging voltage to exceed 16.5 volts. If the battery begins producing gas or boiling violently, reduce the charging rate. Boosting a sulfated battery at a high rate can cause an explosion.

- The A/C system should be serviced using approved refrigerant recovery/recycling equipment. Training in A/C safety precautions and regulations governing the discharging and disposal of automotive chemical refrigerants is essential and required by law.

- Do not expose any part of the A/C system to high temperatures such as an open flame. Excessive heat will increase system pressure and may cause damage to the system.

- Cars equipped with a supplemental restraint system (SRS) automatically deploy airbags in the event of a frontal impact. Airbags are explosive devices. Handled improperly or without adequate safeguards, they can be accidentally activated and cause serious injury.

- Porsche is constantly improving its cars, parts and specifications, often applicable to earlier models. Part numbers listed in this manual are for reference only. Always check with your authorized Porsche dealer parts department for the latest information.

- Use pneumatic and electric tools only to loosen threaded parts and fasteners. Never use these tools to tighten fasteners, especially on light alloy parts. Always use a torque wrench to tighten fasteners to the specified torque.

- The ignition system produces high voltages that can be fatal. Avoid contact with exposed terminals and use extreme care when working on a car with the engine running or the ignition switched on.

- Electronic control module cannot withstand temperatures from a paint-drying booth or a heat lamp in excess of 203 °F (95 °C) and should not be subjected to temperatures in excess of 185 °F (85 °C) for more than two hours.

- Before doing any electrical welding on cars equipped with ABS, disconnect the battery negative (–) terminal (ground cable) and ABS control module connector.

- Disconnecting the battery may erase fault code(s) stored in control module memory. Using special Porsche diagnostic equipment (Bosch "Hammer" or equivalent), check for fault codes prior to disconnecting battery cables.

01 Vehicle Identification and VIN Decoder

Some of the information in this book applies only to cars of a particular model year or range of years. For example, 1994 refers to the 1994 model year but does not necessarily match the calendar year in which the car was manufactured or sold. To be sure of the model year of a particular car, check the Vehicle Identification Number (VIN) on the car.

The VIN is a unique sequence of 17 characters assigned by Porsche to identify each individual car. When decoded, the VIN tells the country and year of manufacture; make, model and serial number; assembly plant and even some equipment specifications.

The Porsche VIN is located on the cowl at the lower left corner of the windshield and on the left door pillar. The 10th character is the model year code. The letters I, O, Q and U are not used for model year designation. Examples: K for 1989, L for 1990, M for 1991 etc. The table below explains some of the codes in the VIN for 1989 through 1994 Porsche 964 covered by this manual.

Sample VIN: W P O A B 2 9 6 8 R S 4 9 9 9 9 9

position   1 2 3 4 5 6 7 8 9 10 11 12 13 14 15 16 17

VIN position	Description	Decoding information	
1	Manufacturing country	W	Germany
2	Manufacturer	P	Dr. Ing. h.c. F. Porshce AG
3	Vehicle type	O	Passenger vehicle
4	Body code	Z A B C	Rest of world (ROW) market Coupe Targa Cabriolet, Speedster
5	Engine code	Z A B C	Rest of world (ROW) market 3.3 liter turbo 3.6 liter naturally aspirated 3.6 liter turbo
6	Airbags	Z 0 2	Rest of world (ROW) market No airbags Airbag equipped
7,8	Model type	96	First two digits of Porsche model (1989 - 1994 911 = 964)
9	Check digit		0 - 9 or X, calculated by NHTSA
10	Model year	K L M N P R	1989 1990 1991 1992 1993 1994
11	Assembly plant	S	Stuttgart, Germany
12	Model type	4	Last digit of Porsche model (1989 - 1994 911 = 964)
13-17	Serial number		Sequential production number specific to each vehicle

02 General

054

GENERAL

The handbook is a quick reference of technical data and technical information for 1989 through 1994 Porsche 964 automobiles. The handbook is divided into seven sections:

0 General, maintenance
1 Engine
2 Engine management
3 Drivetrain
4 Chassis
8 Heating and A/C
9 Electrical

A master listing of repair groups can be found on the inside front cover. A comprehensive index can be found at the back of the handbook.

Vehicle Identification Number (VIN) locations

On cowl at lower left corner of windshield
On left door pillar

See **002 Vehicle Identification and VIN Decoder** for additional VIN information.

Vehicle weights

	Carrera 2	Carrera 4	RS America	Turbo 3.3 & 3.6
Front axle	530 kg (1168 lb)	630 kg (1389 lb)	530 kg (1168 lb)	565 kg (1246 lb)
Rear axle	820 kg (1808 lb)	820 kg (1808 lb)	790 kg (1741 lb)	920 kg (2028 lb)
Total	1350 kg (2976 lb)	1450 kg (3197 lb)	1320 kg (2910 lb)	1485 kg (3274 lb)
Max. front axle	680 kg (1499 lb)	680 kg (1499 lb)	650 kg (1433 lb)	740 kg (1631 lb)
Max. rear axle	995 kg (2184 lb)	1025 kg (2260 lb)	900 kg (1984 lb)	1140 kg (2513 lb)
Max. total	1675 kg (3693 lb)	1705 kg (3759 lb)	1520 kg (3351 lb)	1785 kg (3935 lb)

Engine number code

Stamped on right side of crankcase next to fan housing (**arrow**).

Example:
• **62K00604**

Explanation of digits and letters:
• **6**: 6-cylinder engine
• **2**: Naturally aspirated
• **K**: Model year 1989
• 604th engine installed

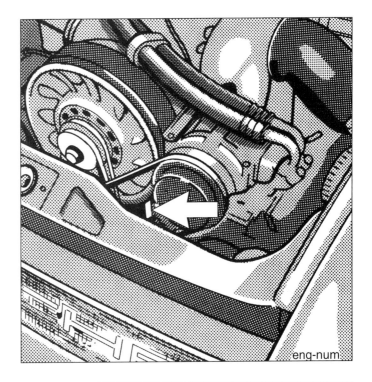

eng-num

No. of cylinders	Engine type	Model year	Serial number
6 6-cylinder engine	**1** 965 Turbo **2** 964 naturally aspirated	**K** 1989 **L** 1990 **M** 1991 **N** 1992 **P** 1993	00001 - 10000 C4 1989 00001 - 50000 C2/C4 1990 00001 - 20000 C2/C4 1991 - 1993 50001 - 60000 C2 Tiptronic 00001 - 05000 Turbo 1991 00001 - 20000 Turbo 1992, 1993

Engine designations

Model year	Type designation	Displacement (cc)	Engine output (kW/HP)	Fuel injection	Models installed
1989	M64/01	3600	184/247	DME	Carrera 4
1990	M64/01	3600	184/247	DME	Carrera 2/4
	M64/02	3600	184/247	DME	Carrera 2 w. Tiptronic
1991	M64/01	3600	184/247	DME	Carrera 2/4
	M64/02	3600	184/247	DME	Carrera 2 w. Tiptronic
	M30/69	3299	235/315	K-Jetronic	Turbo
1992	M64/01	3600	184/247	DME	Carrera 2/4/RS America
	M64/02	3600	184/247	DME	Carrera 2 w. Tiptronic
	M64/03	3600	191/256	DME	RS (not in US models)
	M30/69	3299	235/315	K-Jetronic	Turbo
1993 - 1994	M64/01	3600	184/247	DME	Carrera 2/4/RS America
	M64/02	3600	184/247	DME	Carrera 2 w. Tiptronic
	M64/03	3600	191/256	DME	RS (not in US models)
	M64/50	3600	265/355	K-Jetronic	Turbo

Engine specifications

Engine type	M64/01, M64/02	M64/03	M30/69	M64/50
Bore	100 mm (3.94 in)	100 mm (3.94 in)	97 mm (3.82 in)	100 mm (3.94 in)
Stroke	76.4 mm (3.01 in)	76.4 mm (3.01 in)	74.4 mm (2.93 in)	76.4 mm (3.01 in)
Displacement	3600 cc (219.7 ci)	3600 cc (219.7 ci)	3299 cc (201.3 ci)	3600 cc (219.7 ci)
Compression ratio	11.0 : 1	11.3 : 1	7.0 : 1	7.5 : 1
Kw/HP	184/247	191/256	235/315	265/355
Max. rpm	6700	6800	5750	5500
Fuel grade	90 AKI (95 RON)			
Fuel mileage	19 mpg	19 mpg	16 mpg	16 mpg
Oil pressure at 5000 rpm (oil temperature 90°C/194°F)	5.0 bar (73 psi)		4.5 bar (65 psi)	5.0 bar (73 psi)
Oil consumption	Max. approx. 1.5 liters per 1000 km (1.6 US qt per 621 miles)			

Transmission number code

Bottom of transmission case near drain plug (**arrow**).

Example:
• **G5003 1 L 05641**

Explanation of digits and letters:
• **G5003**: Transmission type G50/03
• **1**: Variant: Normal differential
• **L**: Model year 1990 (not used as of 1992)
• 5641st standard transmission installed

Transmission type	Variants	Model year	Serial number
G50/03 (see table next page)	**0** Without differential **1** Normal differential **2** ZF limited slip differential (M220) **3** Hydraulically controlled limited slip differential (PSD) **4** 40% limited slip differential for RS America models	**K** 1989 **L** 1990 **M** 1991 (no letter used from model year 1992 on)	05641

Transmission and final drive applications

Transmission type	Number of gears	Models installed	Installed from transmission number	Notes
Model year 1989				
G64/00	5	Carrera 4	G6400 3 K 00001	Limited slip differential (PSD)
Z64/00		Carrera 4	Z6400 1 K 00001	Front axle final drive
Model year 1990				
G64/00	5	Carrera 4	G6400 3 L 00001	Limited slip differential (PSD)
Z64/00		Carrera 4	Z6402 1 L 00001	Front axle final drive
G50/03	5	Carrera 2	G5003 1 L 00001	Manual transmission
G50/03	5	Carrera 2	G5003 2 L 00001	Limited slip differential (M220)
A50/01	4	Carrera 2	A5001 1 L 00001	Tiptronic transmission
Model year 1991				
G64/00	5	Carrera 4	G6400 3 M 00001	Limited slip differential (PSD)
G50/03	5	Carrera 2	G5003 1 M 00001	Manual transmission
G50/03	5	Carrera 2	G5003 2 M 00001	Limited slip differential (M220)
G50/03	5	Carrera 2	G5003 2 M 00001	Cup vehicle
A50/01	4	Carrera 2	A5001 1 M 00001	Tiptronic transmission
G50/52	5	Turbo	G5052 1 M 00001	Manual transmission
G50/52	5	Turbo	G5052 2 M 00001	Limited slip differential (M220)
Z64/00		Carrera 4	Z6400 1 M 00001	Front axle final drive
Model years 1992 - 1994				
G64/00	5	Carrera 4	G6400 3 000001	Limited slip differential (PSD)
G50/03	5	Carrera 2	G5003 1 000001	Manual transmission
G50/03	5	Carrera 2	G5003 2 000001	Limited slip differential (M220)
G50/05	5	Carrera 2	G5005 1 000001	Manual transmission
G50/05	5	Carrera 2	G5005 2 000001	Limited slip differential (M220)
A50/03	4	Carrera 2	A5002 1 000001	Tiptronic transmission
G50/05	5	RS America	G5010 2 000001	Limited slip differential (M220)
G50/05	5	RS America	G5010 4 000001	Manual trans. 40% differential
G50/52	5	Turbo	G5052 2 000001	Limited slip differential (M220)
Z64/00		Carrera 4	Z6400 1 000001	Front axle final drive

Jacking points

Front . . . . rear of front wheel body opening
Rear. . . . . front of rear wheel body opening

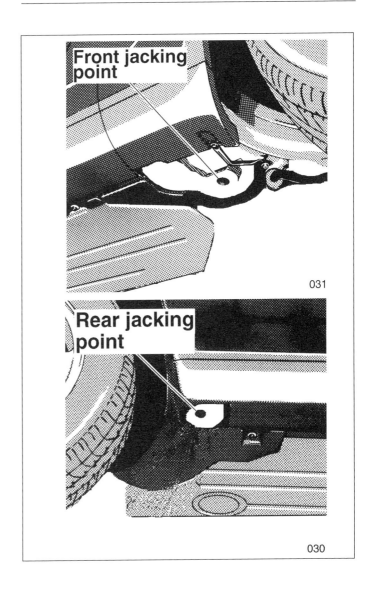

Front jacking point

031

Rear jacking point

030

Tools

Special tools can be purchased through an authorized Porsche dealer or from the following tool manufacturers and/or distributors:

- Assenmacher Specialty Tools, Inc.
  6440 Odell Place, Boulder, CO 80301
  (303) 530-2424   www.asttool.com

- Baum Tools Unlimited, Inc.
  P.O. Box 5867, Sarasota, FL 34277-5867
  (800) 848-6657   www.baumtools.com

- Schley Products, Inc.
  5350 E. Hunter Ave., Anaheim Hills, CA 92807
  (714) 693-7666   www.sptool.com

- Zelenda Automotive, Inc.
  65-60 Austin Street, Forest Hills, NY 11374-4695
  (888) 892-8348   www.zelenda.com

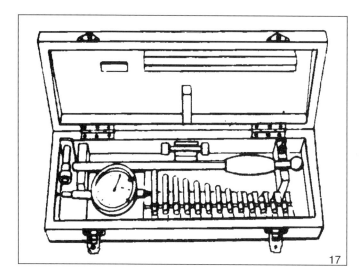

03 Maintenance

0018303b

FLUIDS AND CAPACITIES

Engine oil

Check engine oil level on dipstick with engine running at idle, preferably at operating temperature.

Engine oil capacity
Oil and filter change. . . . . 9 liters (9.5 qt)
Complete refill .11.5 liters (12.5 qt)

Tightening torques
Engine case drain plug . . . . 70 Nm (52 ft-lb)
Oil filter housing drain plug . . . . 31 Nm (23 ft-lb)
Oil thermostat housing drain plug . . . . 65 Nm (48 ft-lb)

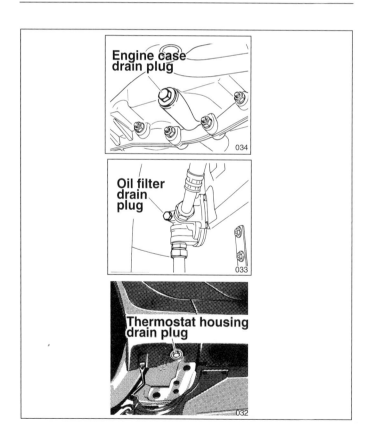

Engine oil viscosity (SAE grade) vs. operating temperature range shown for Porsche engines covered in this manual. Recommended oil viscosity range depends on ambient temperature.

Mineral based oils API SF/CC, SF/CD, SG/CC, SG/CD
Normally above 10°C (50°F) 15 W-40
   alternate 20 W-50
   alternate . . . . .40 W
Normally below 10°C (50°F) 15 W-40
   alternate 10 W-40
   alternate 10 W-30
Normally below -10°C (14°F) 10 W-30
   alternate 5 W-30

Synthetic oils
Normally above 0°C (32°F) 10 W-40
   alternate 15 W-40
   alternate 15 W-50
Normally below 0°C (32°F) 10 W-40
alternate 10 W-30
alternate 5 W-30

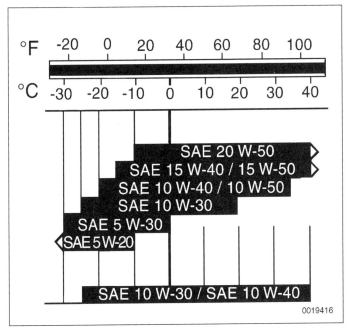

0019416

Transmission and final drive lubricants

Transmission and final drive oils
Manual transmission . . . . 75 W 90
  Mineral based oil . . . . , API classification GL5
  Synthetic oil . . . . MIL-L 2105 B
Automatic transmission oil (ATF) . . . . .Dexron II D

Transmission and final drive oils capacities
C2 (manual). . . . . .3.6 liters (3.8 qt)
C4 front final drive . . . . .1.2 liters (1.27 qt)
C4 . . . . .3.8 liters (3.9 qt)
Turbo . . . . .3.7 liters (3.9 qt)
Tiptronic final drive . . . . .0.9 liters (1.0 qt)

Tiptronic transmission capacity (Dexron II D)
Complete refill . . . . .9.0 liters (9.5 qt)
Oil change only . . . . .3.0 liters (3.2 qt)

Brake fluid, power steering fluid

Brake fluid specification
Fluid capacity
  Brake hydraulics
    C2 . . . . .0.34 liter (0.72 pt)
    C4/Turbo . . . . .0.75 liter (1.59 pt)
  Brake booster circuit (ABS). . . . . approx. 1.6 liter (1.7 qt)
Recommended fluid DOT4

Service note –
- 1993 and later models: Use DOT4-Plus brake fluid (Porsche part no. 000 043 202 04).
- Porsche DOT 4-Plus brake fluid has a higher boiling point than standard DOT4 fluid.

Power steering fluid
Dexron II D . . . . .1.0 liter (1.06 qt)

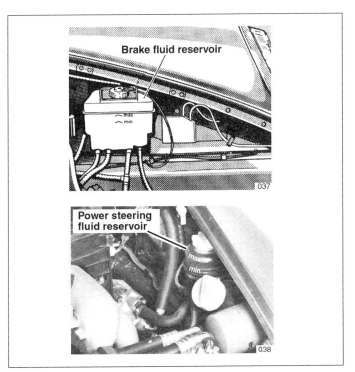

Brake fluid reservoir

037

Power steering fluid reservoir

038

Air conditioner (A/C)

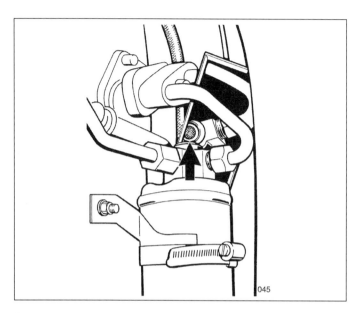

Service note –

- Use sight glass (**arrow**) to check refrigerant charge. Air bubbles indicate low freon charge.

A/C refrigerant and oil capacities

R12 refrigerant (1989 - 1992) . . . . 930 g (30 oz)
R134a refrigerant (1993 - 1994) . . . . 840 g (27 oz)
Compressor oil:
   R12 refrigerant (1989 - 1992)
    Densoil . . . . .100 ± 20 cm^3 (3.4 ± 0.7 oz)
   R134a refrigerant (1993 - 1994)
    ND 8 . . . . .140 ± 20 cm^3 (4.7 ± 0.7 oz)

A/C lines tightening torques

5/8" outside threads. . . . . 17 ± 3 Nm (13 ± 2 ft-lb)
3/4" outside threads. . . . . 24 ± 4 Nm (18 ± 3 ft-lb)
7/8" outside threads. . . . . 33 ± 4 Nm (24 ± 3 ft-lb)

Tires

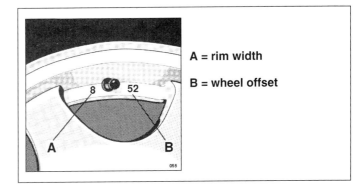

A = rim width

B = wheel offset

Tire pressures with standard tires

205/55 ZR 16	2.5 bar (36 psi)
225/50 ZR 16	3.0 bar (44 psi)
205/50 ZR 17	2.5 bar (36 psi)
255/40 ZR 17	2.5 bar (36 psi)

Standard tire sizes

C2/C4 front	205/55 ZR 16
C2/C4 rear	225/50 ZR 16
Turbo/turbo look front	205/50 ZR 17
Turbo/turbo look rear	255/40 ZR 17

Optional tire sizes

C2/C4 front	205/50 ZR 17
C2/C4 rear	255/40 ZR 17

ENGINE MAINTENANCE

Air filter housing

Remove oil filler cap.

Release all 4 retaining clips (**arrows**) before removing outer housing.

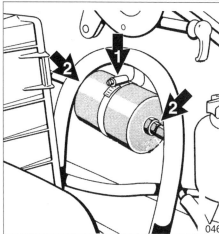

Fuel filter

Release clamp **1**.

Release pressure fittings **2**.

Air and fuel filters

- Install air filter element with fins in horizontal position.
- When removing fuel filter, have shop towel ready to catch spilled fuel.
- When installing fuel filter, arrow on filter housing shows direction of fuel flow.

Valve adjustment

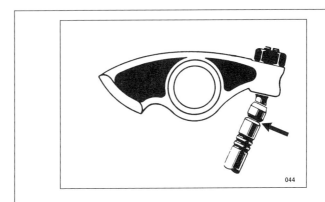

Valve clearance (arrow)

Intake valves . . . . .0.1 mm (0.004 in)
Exhaust valves . . . . .0.1 mm (0.004 in)

Valve adjustment (cont.)

Service note –

- Adjust valves clearance with engine cold (approx. 20°C/68°F).
- Drain engine oil from crankcase.
- Remove heater blower elbow and hose, air filter cover and element.
- Detach A/C compressor from its mount without disconnecting A/C lines.
- Remove upper and lower valve covers.
- Using marks on ignition rotor, TDC mark on crankshaft pulley, and firing order information on following pages, set engine to TDC for each cylinder to adjust valves for that cylinder.
- Place feeler gauge between valve stem and valve adjusting screw cap.

Top dead center (TDC)

Service note –

- ZL mark on crankshaft pulley aligned with mark on blower housing indicates TDC, Cyl. 1.
- With crankshaft pulley at TDC, distributor rotors must align with marks (**arrows**) on distributor bodies.
- If distributor **A** rotor is aligned but distributor **B** rotor is not, try to turn distributor **B** rotor by hand. If rotor turns freely, drive belt in lower distributor housing is broken.

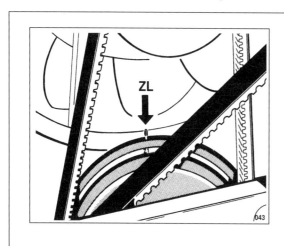

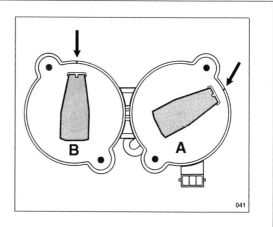

Firing order

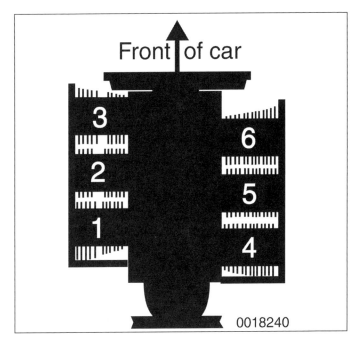

0018240

Service note –

- To determine start of firing order, inspect lip of ignition distributor body for cylinder 1 scribe mark.
- Ignition rotor rotates clockwise.
- Cylinder 1 is at left rear when viewing engine from rear of engine compartment.

Ignition firing order
- All models 1-6-2-4-3-5

Drive belts, Carrera 2 / 4

In Carrera 2 / 4 models, a pair of V-belts are used to drive alternator and cooling fan.

Service note –

• Adjust V-belt tension by moving adjusting shims to inside or outside of pulley halves.

Tightening torques

Pulley **A** (M6 Allen) . . . . 10 Nm (7.5 ft-lb)
Pulley **B** nut . . . . 50 Nm (37 ft-lb)

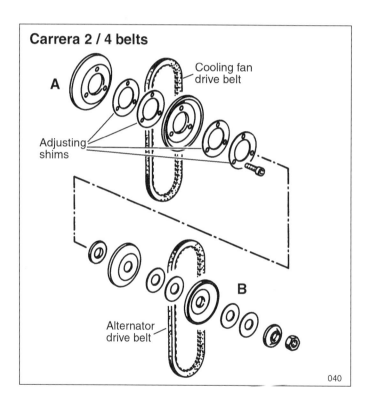

Carrera 2 / 4 belts

A

Cooling fan
drive belt

Adjusting
shims

B

Alternator
drive belt

040

A/C compressor drive belt, Carrera 2 / 4

V-belt is used to drive Carrera 2 / 4 A/C compressor.

Service note –

• To adjust A/C belt tension:
  -Loosen A/C compressor mounting bolts (**A**).
  -Use compressor positioning bolt (**B**) to adjust belt tension.

Tightening torque

A/C compressor to compressor mount . . . 22 Nm (17 ft-lb)

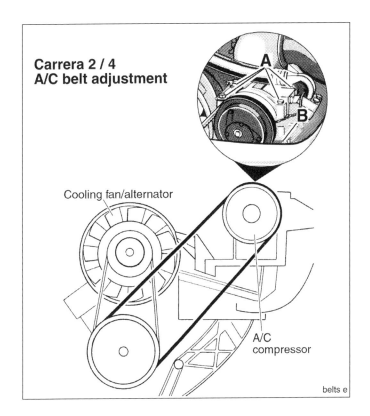

Carrera 2 / 4
A/C belt adjustment

Cooling fan/alternator

A/C
compressor

belts e

Drive belts, Turbo models

Turbo models use a V-belt to drive the cooling fan and a polyribbed belt to drive the alternator and A/C compressor.

Service note –

- Adjust V-belt tension by moving adjusting shims to inside or outside of pulley halves.
- Relieve polyribbed belt tension by pivoting belt tensioner.

Tightening torques

V-belt pulley bolt (M6 Allen). . . . . .10 Nm (7.5 ft-lb)
Polyribbed belt pulley nut. . . . . 50 Nm (37 ft-lb)

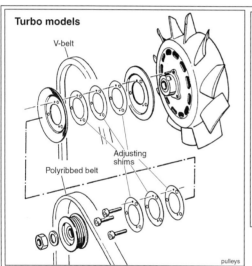

Turbo models

V-belt

Adjusting shims

Polyribbed belt

pulleys

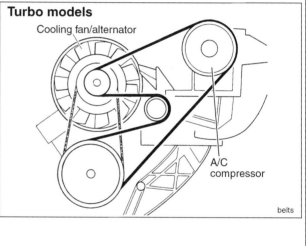

Turbo models

Cooling fan/alternator

A/C compressor

belts

Power steering belt

Power steering pump is driven by toothed wheel at rear of right camshaft (front of car side of engine). Drive belt is accessible from underside of vehicle, right front of engine. For more details, see **48 Steering**.

Air pump belt

Belt tension specification
Belt deflection
with light thumb pressure . . . . 6 - 8 mm (0.25 - 0.3 in)

Service note –
- To adjust air pump belt:
  - Loosen lock bolt (**arrow**) slightly.
  - Turn self-locking allen bolt for correct belt tension.
  - Tighten lock bolt.

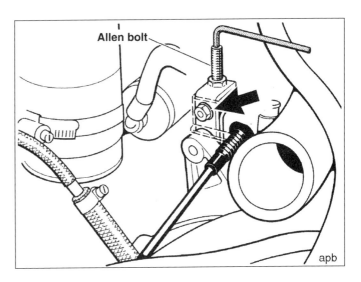

Allen bolt

apb

TESTING FAULT MEMORY

Diagnostic plug

Service note –

- Use Porsche 9288 tester ("Bosch Hammer") or KTS 301 Bosch tester to access fault memory at 19-pin (ISO standard) diagnostic plug.
- Alternatively, use flashing code tester 9268 and adapter lead 9268/2 to access DME fault memory at diagnostic plug.
- 1991 and later US models: Use Check Engine Light to check for fault codes:

  -If Check Engine light is illuminated, emission-related faults can be 'read out' by interpreting the flashes or blinks of the light. Depressing the accelerator pedal with engine not running and the ignition on for 3 seconds will start the read out. Consult the **24 DME Fuel Injection** for fault code information.

Diagnostic plug location
Behind right side footwell trim

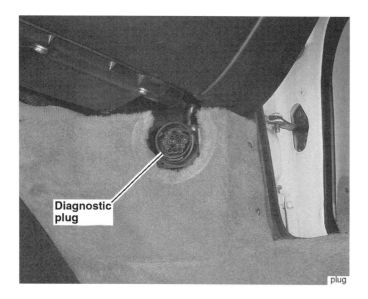

Diagnostic plug

plug

System testing

Carrera 2 / Carrera 4/ RS America systems that can be tested from diagnostic plug:
- DME
- Air conditioning and heating system
- Airbag system
- Tiptronic transmission control

Additional systems not listed require special break out adapters. Rear spoiler control and central locking are not testable.

Turbo model systems that can be tested from diagnostic plug:
- Oxygen sensor control unit
- Turbocharger control unit
- Acceleration enrichment control unit
- Ignition control unit
- Airbag system

MAINTENANCE SCHEDULE

Maintenance item / Mileage	7,500	15,000	22,500	30,000	37,500	45,000	52,500	60,000	67,500	75,000	82,500
Check fault memory readout		✳		✳		✳		✳		✳	
Change engine oil and filter	✳	✳	✳	✳	✳	✳	✳	✳	✳	✳	✳
Check and adjust valve clearance		✳		✳		✳		✳		✳	
Check and adjust engine drive belts		✳		✳		✳		✳		✳	
Replace spark plugs				✳				✳			
Replace auxiliary air pump filter				✳				✳			
Replace engine air filter element				✳				✳			
Check operation of resonance flap				✳				✳			
Check crankcase ventilation hoses		✳		✳		✳		✳		✳	
Inspect fuel system for leaks		✳		✳		✳		✳		✳	
Check intake system for leaks				✳				✳			
Inspect exhaust system for leaks		✳		✳		✳		✳		✳	
Check engine and transmission for leaks	✳	✳	✳	✳	✳	✳	✳	✳	✳	✳	✳
Change Tiptronic transmission oil				✳				✳			
Change front final drive oil (C4)								✳			
Change Tiptronic final drive oil								✳			
Check oil level in standard transmission	✳	✳	✳	✳	✳	✳	✳	✳	✳	✳	✳
Change standard transmission gear oil								✳			
Check clutch operation and free play		✳		✳		✳		✳		✳	
Bleed and flush brake fluid	Every 2 years. 1993 and later models: Every 3 years										
Check and adjust parking brake		✳		✳		✳		✳		✳	
Inspect brake pads/rotors for wear		✳		✳		✳		✳		✳	
Check steering rack components for wear		✳		✳		✳		✳		✳	
Check condition of power steering belt				✳				✳			
Inspect power steering system for leaks				✳				✳			
Check ball joints and A-arm bushings for wear				✳				✳			
Inspect C/V joint boots for damage		✳		✳		✳		✳		✳	
Check C/V joints for wear		✳		✳		✳		✳		✳	
Check tire pressures and tread depth	✳	✳	✳	✳	✳	✳	✳	✳	✳	✳	✳
Lubricate door hinges		✳		✳		✳		✳		✳	
Check door latches and check-rod operation		✳		✳		✳		✳		✳	
Check door, hood and rear deck locks		✳		✳		✳		✳		✳	
Check seat belt operation				✳				✳			
Check operation of lights, horns and wiper motor	✳	✳	✳	✳	✳	✳	✳	✳	✳	✳	✳
Check washer fluid level, aim washer nozzles	✳	✳	✳	✳	✳	✳	✳	✳	✳	✳	✳
Check intensive windshield cleaning system	✳	✳	✳	✳	✳	✳	✳	✳	✳	✳	✳

MAINTENANCE SCHEDULE

Maintenance item \ Mileage	7,500	15,000	22,500	30,000	37,500	45,000	52,500	60,000	67,500	75,000	82,500
Check and aim headlights				✳				✳			
Check operation of accelerator linkage				✳				✳			
Check door, hood and rear deck weather strip		✳		✳		✳		✳		✳	
Check and correct battery electrolyte level	✳	✳	✳	✳	✳	✳	✳	✳	✳	✳	✳
Check operation of all electrical equipment		✳		✳		✳		✳		✳	
Check operation of A/C, heater and ventilation systems		✳		✳		✳		✳		✳	
Replace fuel filter								✳			
During road test											
Check operation of service and parking brakes		✳		✳		✳		✳		✳	
Check kick-down operation (Tiptronic only)		✳		✳		✳		✳		✳	
Check operation of transmission locking units		✳		✳		✳		✳		✳	
Inspect for leaks after road test	✳	✳	✳	✳	✳	✳	✳	✳	✳	✳	✳

10 Engine Crankcase

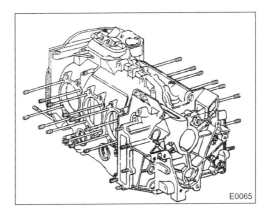

E0065

10

CRANKCASE

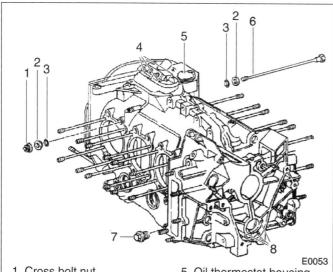

E0053

1. Cross bolt nut
2. Cross bolt washer
3. Cross bolt seal
4. Crankcase breather cover
   fasteners
5. Oil thermostat housing
6. Cross bolt
7. Oil drain plug
8. Intermediate shaft cover
   fasteners

Tightening torques

Crankcase breather cover
  to crankcase (M6) . . . . .10 Nm (7.5 ft-lb)
Crankcase cross bolt/nut (M10) . . . . 50 Nm (37 ft-lb)
Crankcase nut/bolt (M8) . . . . 23 Nm (17 ft-lb)
Drain plug to crankcase (M20) . . . . 70 Nm (52 ft-lb)
Intermediate shaft cover
  to crankcase (M6) . . . . .10 Nm (7.5 ft-lb)
Relief valve cap to crankcase (M18) . . . . . 60 Nm (44 ft-lb)

Cross bolts and seals

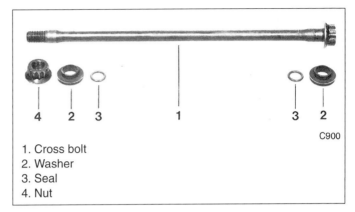

1. Cross bolt
2. Washer
3. Seal
4. Nut

Crankcase cross bolts, seals, washers and nuts have been modified numerous times over the years. Check with an authorized Porsche parts department for latest updates on these parts.

Bore specifications

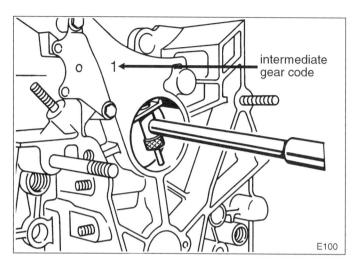

intermediate gear code

E100

Service note –

• Crankshaft main bearings are available in standard size and oversize (see table below).
• If case bores are larger than 65.019 mm (2.560 in), ream bores and use oversize bearing set.
• If crankcase has worn or damaged intermediate bearing bores, case must be replaced.

Location	Specification	Wear limit
Main bearing bore:		
Standard	65.000 - 65.019 mm (2.559 - 2.560 in)	0.019 mm (0.0007 in)
Oversize	65.250 - 65.269 mm (2.569 - 2.570 in)	0.019 mm (0.0007 in)
Intermediate shaft:		
Bore 1	27.500 - 27. 521 mm (1.0827 - 1.0835 in)	0.021 mm (0.0008 in)
Bore 2	26.500 - 26.521 mm (1.043 - 1.044 in)	0.021 mm (0.0008 in)

Cylinder head studs

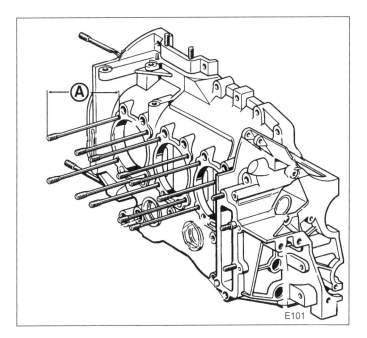

E101

Service note –

• Use Loctite® 270 to secure cylinder head studs in place.

Cylinder head stud

Projected length **A** . . . . . 130.20 - 0.50 mm (5.13 - 0.02 in)

Oil pressure relief valves

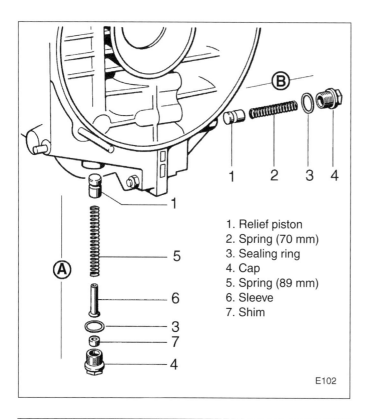

1. Relief piston
2. Spring (70 mm)
3. Sealing ring
4. Cap
5. Spring (89 mm)
6. Sleeve
7. Shim

E102

Oil pressure relief valve spring lengths

Relief valve **A**. . . . . 89 mm (3.504 in)
Relief valve **B**. . . . . 70 mm (2.756 in)

Note–

• An additional oil pressure relief valve is installed in top of oil tank. See **17 Lubrication**.

13 Crankshaft

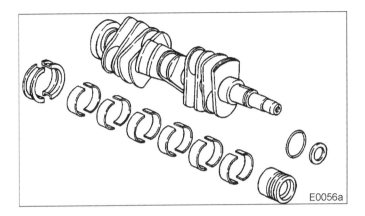

E0056a

CRANKSHAFT AND INTERMEDIATE SHAFT

Crankshaft—general

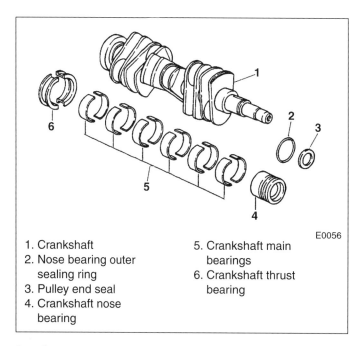

E0056

1. Crankshaft
2. Nose bearing outer sealing ring
3. Pulley end seal
4. Crankshaft nose bearing
5. Crankshaft main bearings
6. Crankshaft thrust bearing

Service note –

- If scoring has occurred at front or rear sealing surfaces of crankshaft, machine seal journals.
- Oversized pulley end (nose bearing) seal is available from Porsche.
- Oversized flywheel end seal is not available.

Crankshaft tolerance group

Blue paint dot	0.25 mm (0.010 in)
Green paint dot	0.50 mm (0.020 in)

Crankshaft journal specifications

Journal	Diameter

Main bearing journals 1 - 7
   standard
   0.25 mm (0.010 in) oversize
   0.50 mm (0.020 in) oversize
	
	59.971 - 59.990 mm (2.361 - 2.362 in)
	59.721 - 59.740 mm (2.351 - 2.352 in)
	59.471 - 59.490 mm (2.341 - 2.342 in)

Main bearing journal 8
   standard
   0.25 mm (0.010 in) oversize
   0.50 mm (0.020 in) oversize
	
	30.980 - 30.993 mm (1.219 - 1.220 in)
	30.730 - 30.743 mm (1.209 - 1.210 in)
	30.480 - 30.493 mm (1.200 - 1.201 in)

Connecting rod journals
   standard
   0.25 mm (0.010 in) oversize
   0.50 mm (0.020 in) oversize
	
	54.971 - 54.990 mm (2.164 - 2.165 in)
	54.721 - 54.740 mm (2.154 - 2.155 in)
	54.471 - 54.490 mm (2.144 - 2.145 in)

Crankshaft seal journals
   pulley end
   flywheel end
	
	29.960 - 29.993 mm (1.179 - 1.181 in)
	89.780 - 90.000 mm (3.535 - 3.543 in)

Crankshaft journals
   timing chain sprocket
   distributor drive gear
	
	42.002 - 42.013 mm (1.653 - 1.654 in)
	42.002 - 42.013 mm (1.653 - 1.654 in)

Crankshaft runout checked at main journals 4 & 8	Maximum 0.04 mm (0.0016 in)

Crankshaft journal wear limits

Journal	Clearance	Wear limit
Main bearings 1-7	0.010 - 0.072 mm (0.0004 - 0.0028 in)	59.960 mm (2.360 in)
Main bearing 8	0.048 - 0.104 mm (0.0018 to 0.004 in)	30.970 mm (1.219 in)
Connecting rod bearing	0.030 - 0.088 mm (0.0011 - 0.0034 in)	54.960 mm (2.163 in)

Seal journal
   pulley end
   flywheel end
	
	-
	-
		
		29.670 mm (1.168 in)
		89.580 mm (3.526 in)

Distributor and intermediate shaft drive gears

Service note –

• With circlip installed there must be no clearance between distributor drive gear and circlip.
• Most common circlip for initial setup is 2.3 mm (0.091 in) See table below for circlip thickness color codes.

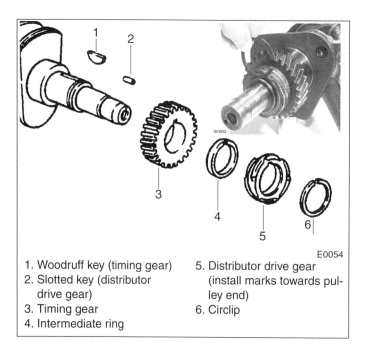

E0054

1. Woodruff key (timing gear)
2. Slotted key (distributor drive gear)
3. Timing gear
4. Intermediate ring
5. Distributor drive gear (install marks towards pulley end)
6. Circlip

Thickness	Color code	Porsche p/n
2.1 mm (0.083 in)	Black	901 102 148 03
2.2 mm (0.087 in)	Yellow / brown	901 102 148 02
2.3 mm (0.091 in)	Blue	901 102 148 01
2.4 mm (0.094 in)	Bright	901 102 148 00

Intermediate shaft and gears

Timing chain sprockets (**4**) are available as replacement parts.

Service note –

- Removal: Note orientation and position marks. Press off shaft.
- Installation: Heat on hot plate. Press to stop. Observe orientation marks.

Intermediate shaft drive gear (**6**) is a complete assembly integral with intermediate shaft.

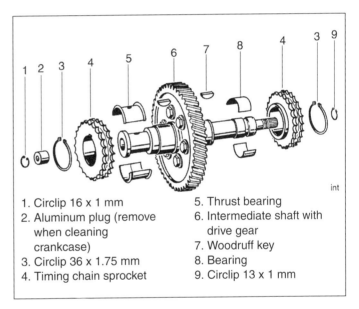

int

1. Circlip 16 x 1 mm
2. Aluminum plug (remove when cleaning crankcase)
3. Circlip 36 x 1.75 mm
4. Timing chain sprocket
5. Thrust bearing
6. Intermediate shaft with drive gear
7. Woodruff key
8. Bearing
9. Circlip 13 x 1 mm

Intermediate Shaft Wear Limits

Intermediate shaft end play	0.030 - 0.084 mm (0.0012 - 0.0033 in)
Intermediate shaft axial play	0.040 - 0.133 mm (0.0016 - 0.0052 in)
Intermediate shaft thrust bearing (**5**) diameter (crankshaft pulley end)	25.000 - 24.980 mm (0.984 - 0.983 in)
Intermediate shaft bearing (**8**) diameter (flywheel end)	23.98 - 23.967 mm (0.944 - 0.943 in)

CRANKSHAFT PULLEY

Crankshaft pulley, removing

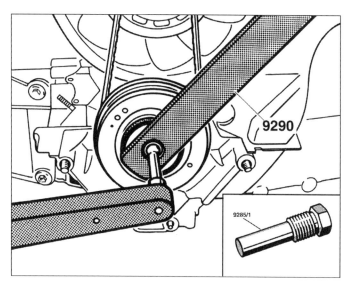

Service note –
- Remove and reinstall crankshaft pulley (harmonic balancer) bolt by counterholding pulley with special tool 9290.
- To remove pulley, screw special tool 9285/1 into outer pulley threads.
- Before reassembly:
  - Thoroughly degrease crankshaft and pulley tapered surfaces.
  - Lubricate crankshaft pulley bolt head mating surface and threads with thin coat of oil.

Caution–
- Do not damage harmonic balancer through excessive hammering or prying during removal or installation.
- Do not disturb Allen bolts visible through recessed front of pulley.

Tightening torque
Crankshaft pulley to crankshaft (M14) . . 235 Nm (173 ft-lb)

Crankshaft pulley, straightening

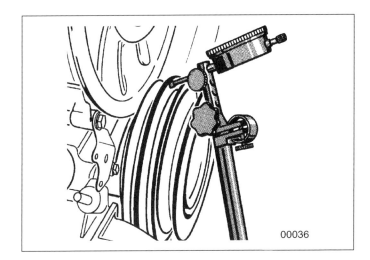

Service note –

- Measure crankshaft pulley runout with micrometer at outer pulley lip.
- If run-out exceeds maximum allowable 0.5 mm (0.019 in), straighten by tapping inside shell of pulley with soft faced hammer and recheck.

CONNECTING RODS

Service note –

- Always replace connecting rod bolts and nuts.
- Check wrist pin fit to small end bushing. Wrist pin should slide through bushing with light finger pressure.
- Check that numbers stamped on side of connecting rod cap and rod body match (cap and rod are matched set).
- Final two digits marked on shank of replacement connecting rod are its weight class code.
- Weigh complete connecting rod, without bearing shells.
- Difference in rod weights must not exceed 9 grams.
- Sort connecting rods into 3 pairs:
  -Install heaviest pair at cylinders 3 and 6.
  -Install next heaviest pair at cylinders 2 and 5.
  -Install lightest at cylinders 1 and 4.
  -If original set of connecting rods was balanced to factory specifications, this step will give engine near perfect balance.

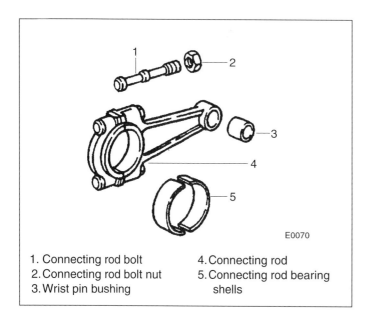

1. Connecting rod bolt
2. Connecting rod bolt nut
3. Wrist pin bushing
4. Connecting rod
5. Connecting rod bearing shells

Connecting rod weight classes

Connecting rods are marked (**arrow**) with two digit designation (last two digits of Porsche part no.) indicating weight-group.

Example: Connecting rod with part no. 964 103 020 56 is stamped "56", belongs to weight class 3, weighs 642 - 651 grams.

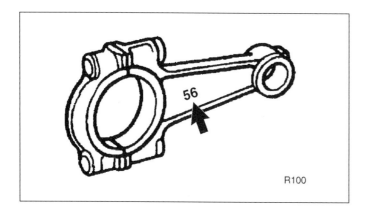

Designation	Weight class	Weight
53	3	615 - 624 grams
54	4	624 - 633 grams
55	5	633 - 642 grams
56	6	642 - 651 grams
57	7	651 - 660 grams
58	8	660 - 669 grams
59	9	669 - 678 grams
60	10	678 - 687 grams
61	11	687 - 696 grams

Connecting rod specifications

Connecting rod dimensions
Crankshaft bore. 58.000 - 58.019 mm (2.2835 - 2.2842 in)
Wrist pin bore . . . . 23.020 - 23.033 mm (0.906 - 0.907 in)

Service note –
• Always tighten connecting rod fasteners in stages.

Tightening torques
M9 x 1.25 bolt head marked with **00**
   stage I . . . . 20 Nm (14 ft-lb)
   stage II . . . . plus 90° (¼ turn)
M9 x 1.25 bolt head marked with **12.9**
stage I . . . . 15 Nm (11 ft-lb)
stage II. . . . . plus 90° (¼ turn)
stage III . . . . plus 90° (¼ turn)

Connecting rod bolts

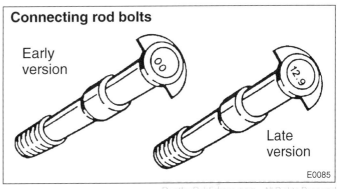

Early version

Late version

E0085

PISTONS AND CYLINDERS

Service note –

- Weigh pistons with wrist pins and circlips.
- Always replace wrist pin locking circlips. Use special tool 9500 - 9500/1 to install.
- Do not mix wrist pins and pistons. Keep pin/piston together as matched set.
- Check cylinder roundness by measuring bore in two directions perpendicular to stud holes.
- Follow manufacturer's instructions for piston orientation during assembly.

Piston/cylinder running clearance

Maximum . . . . .0.08 mm (0.0031 in)
Wall clearance
C2/C4, RS America,
Turbo 3.6 . . . . 0.02 - 0.03 mm (0.0008 - 0.0012 in)
Turbo 3.3 . . . . 0.053 - 0.077 mm (0.002 - 0.003 in)

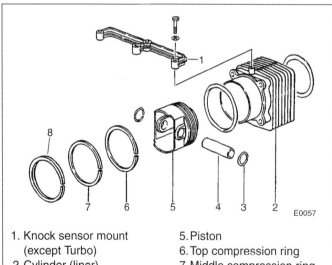

E0057

1. Knock sensor mount (except Turbo)
2. Cylinder (liner)
3. Wrist pin circlip
4. Wrist pin
5. Piston
6. Top compression ring
7. Middle compression ring
8. Oil control ring

Piston crown markings (C2, C4, RS America)

Piston crown is marked as follows (right to left):

- Tolerance group (size and weight)
- Manufacturer's mark
- E (always install toward intake port)

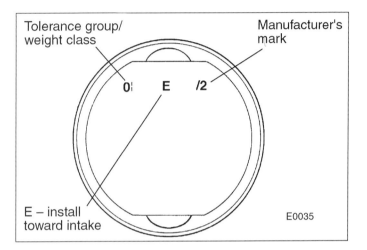

Tolerance group/
weight class

Manufacturer's
mark

0   E   /2

E – install
toward intake

E0035

Piston and cylinder size groups

(C2, C4, RS America, Turbo 3.6)

Tolerance group	Cylinder diameter	Piston diameter
0	100.000 - 100.007 mm (3.9370 - 3.9373 in)	99.970 - 99.980 mm (3.9358 - 3.9362 in)
1	100.007 - 100.014 mm (3.9373 - 3.9376 in)	99.977 - 99.987 mm (3.9361 - 3.9365 in)
2	100.014 - 100.021 mm (3.9376 - 3.9378 in)	99.984 - 99.994 mm (3.9364 - 3.9368 in)
3	100.021 - 100.028 mm (3.9378 - 3.9381 in)	99.991 - 100.001 mm (3.9367 - 3.9370 in)

Piston weight classes

(C2, C4, RS America, Turbo 3.6)

Symbol for piston weight class identification may be stamped vertically next to size class symbol.

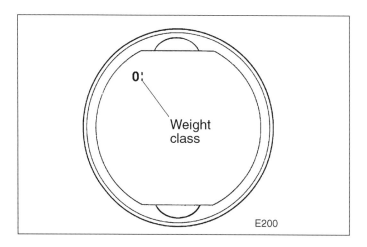

Engine code	Class	Weight (grams)
M 64/01, M 64/02, M 64/03	- / - - + / +	644 - 652 652 - 660
M 64/50	- / - - + / ++	584 - 592 592 - 600
M 30/69	- - - + ++	616 - 620 620 - 624 624 - 628 628 - 632

Measuring cylinder

Service note –

- Measure cylinder height (**H**) and diameter (**D**).
- Check cylinder bore wear by measuring 56 mm (2.20 in) below upper sealing surface.
- Specifications and wear tolerances given on following page.

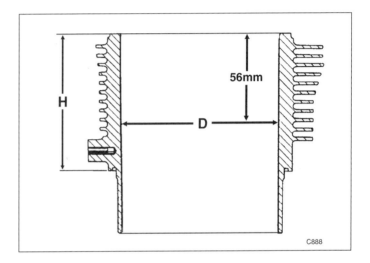

Cylinder sizes, cylinder height

Cylinder manufacturer and dimensions indicated by marks on base of cylinder, opposite knock sensor mounting boss.

Number on right indicates cylinder size code (diameter).

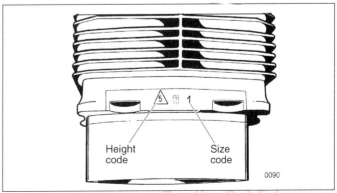

Height code

Size code

	Turbo 3.3		C2, C4, RS America, Turbo 3.6	
Size Code	Cylinder diameter	Piston diameter	Cylinder diameter	Piston diameter
0	95.000 - 95.010 mm (3.7402 - 3.7406 in)	94.933 - 94.947 mm (3.7375 - 3.7381 in)	100.000 - 100.007 mm (3.9370 - 3.9373 in)	99.970 - 99.980 mm (3.9358 - 3.9362 in)
1	95.010 - 95.020 mm (3.7406 - 3.7409 in)	94.943 - 94.957 mm (3.7379 - 3.7385 in)	100.007 - 100.014 mm (3.9373 - 3.9376 in)	99.977 - 99. 987 mm (3.9361 - 3.9365 in)
2	95.020 - 95.030 mm (3.7409 - 3.7413 in)	94.953 - 94.967 mm (3.7383 - 3.7389 in)	100.014 - 100.021 mm (3.9376 - 3.9378 in)	99.984 - 9.994 mm (3.9364 - 3.9368 in)
3			100.021 - 100.028 mm (3.9378 - 3.9381 in)	99.991 - 100.001 mm (3.9367 - 3.9371)

Height code	Height
⑤	82.750 - 0.020 mm (3.2578 - 0.0008 in)
⑥	82.770 - 0.020 mm (3.2587 - 0.0008 in)

Service note –

• Be sure to install cylinders of same height (code 5 or 6) in same cylinder bank of engine.

Piston rings

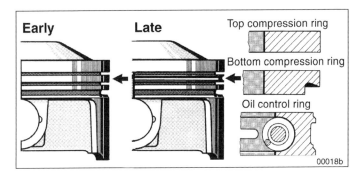

Note differences between ring supports for top and bottom compression ring gaps (**arrows**) on early piston (1989 C2/C4 models) and late piston (1990 on). This design change reduces engine oil consumption and blow-by.

Piston ring	End gap (new)	Wear limit	Side clearance	Wear limit
Top compression ring	0.15 - 0.3 mm (0.006 - 0.012 in)	0.8 mm (0.031 in)	0.070 - 0.102 mm (0.0028 - 0.0040 in)	0.2 mm (0.0078 in)
Bottom compression ring			0.040 - 0.072 mm (0.0016 - 0.0028 in)	
Oil control ring	0.15 - 0.3 mm (0.006 - 0.012 in)	1.0 mm (0.039 in)	0.020 - 0.052 mm (0.0008 - 0.0020 in)	0.1 mm (0.0039 in)

FLYWHEEL

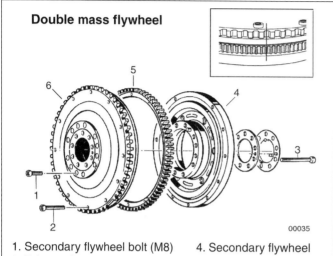

Double mass flywheel

1. Secondary flywheel bolt (M8)
2. Primary flywheel bolt (M7)
3. Flywheel to crankshaft (M10)
4. Secondary flywheel
5. Starter ring gear
6. Primary flywheel

00035

Service note –

• If rattle is present at idle or in decel/load mode, check double-mass flywheel.
• To determine if double-mass flywheel is damaged, turn ring gear in either direction. If it turns more than 15 mm (0.6 in) without moving crankshaft, flywheel is faulty.

To facilitate double mass flywheel reassembly, scribe relative position of parts (see inset) prior to disassembly.

Tightening torques

Clutch pressure plate to lightweight
("cup") flywheel (always replace). . . . . . . 24 Nm (18 ft-lb)
Flywheel to crankshaft (always replace)
Single mass (1989 C4) . . . . 90 Nm (66 ft-lb)
Double mass (1990 on). . . . . 85 Nm (63 ft-lb)
Primary flywheel (always replace)
to cover plate. . . . . 22 Nm (16 ft-lb)
Primary flywheel (always replace)
to secondary flywheel . . . . 35 Nm (26 ft-lb)

15 Cylinder Heads, Camshafts, Timing Chains

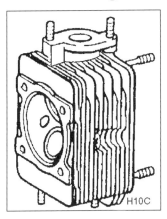

H10C

CYLINDER HEADS

This repair group provides reconditioning information for the cylinder heads, including valve train reconditioning specifications.

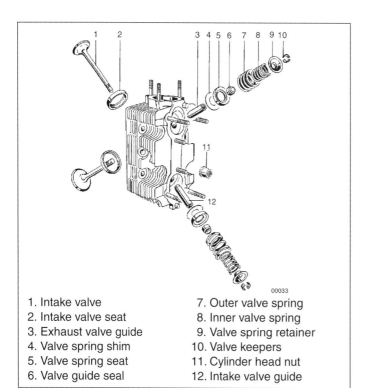

00033

1. Intake valve	7. Outer valve spring
2. Intake valve seat	8. Inner valve spring
3. Exhaust valve guide	9. Valve spring retainer
4. Valve spring shim	10. Valve keepers
5. Valve spring seat	11. Cylinder head nut
6. Valve guide seal	12. Intake valve guide

Service note –

• Cylinder head repair and reconditioning require that the engine be removed from the car and disassembled on an appropriate engine stand.

Tightening torques

Camshaft housing
  to cylinder head (M8). . . . . 23 Nm (17 ft-lb)
Chain sprocket to camshaft . . . . 120 Nm (88 ft-lb)
Cylinder head to crankcase(C2, C4, RS, 3.6 Turbo)
  stage 1. . . . . 20 Nm (11 ft-lb)
  stage 2 (torque angle) . . . . 90° ± 2°
Cylinder head to crankcase (3.3 Turbo)
  stage 1. . . . . 15 Nm (11 ft-lb)
  stage 2 (torque angle) . . . . 90° ± 2°

Tightening torques (cont.)

Knock sensor bridge to cylinder (M6) . . . . .9.7 Nm (7 ft-lb)
Knock sensor to bridge (M8) . . . . . 20 ± 5 Nm (15 ± 4 ft-lb)
NTC sensor to cylinder head . . . . . 10 - 12 Nm (7 - 9 ft-lb)
Rocker shaft to cylinder head (M7) . . . . . . 20 Nm (15 ft-lb)
Spark plug (M14) to
    cylinder head . . . . 20 - 30 Nm (15 - 22 ft-lb)
Timing chain housing cover
    to housing . . . . .5.5 Nm (4 ft-lb)
Timing chain housing to crankcase. . . . . . 23 Nm (17 ft-lb)

Cylinder head nuts, tightening

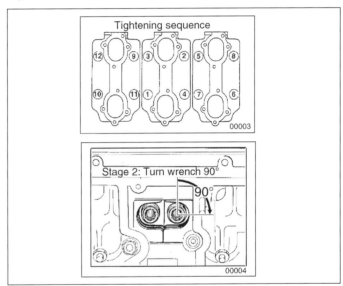

Tightening sequence

00003

Stage 2: Turn wrench 90°

90°

00004

Service note –

• Coat cylinder head stud and nut contact surface with Op-
  timoly® HT (copper paste) prior to installation.
• For head nut tightening sequence, see illustration.
• Head nuts are tightened in two stages. Stage 2 is illustrated. (Also see torque table above.)

Cylinder head machining

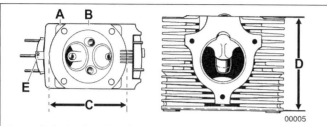

A	Cylinder head surface
B	Cylinder head surface
C	Diameter of machined surface = 145 mm (5.709 in)
D	Cylinder head hgt.= 84.48 ± 0.02 mm (3.326 ± 0.0008 in)

Service note –

- Machine cylinder head surfaces **A** and **B** equal amounts.
- Cylinder head surface may only be machined twice.
- Always machine complete bank (groups of three) cylinder heads to same dimension.
- Bevel edges of machined surfaces slightly.
- Mark cylinder head port area (**E**) with –0.10 mm (0.004 in) or -0.20 mm (0.008 in) to indicate that head was machined.

Machining specifications

Mill surfaces **A** and **B** equally . . . . .0.10 mm (0.004 in)
Maximum metal that can be
  removed from cylinder head . . . . 0.20 ± 0.02 mm
                                                         (0.008 ± 0.0008 in)
Diameter (**C**) of milled surface . . . . 145 mm (5.709 in)
Height (**D**) of new
cylinder head . . . . . . 84.48 ± 0.02 mm (3.326 ± 0.0008 in)

VALVE GUIDES AND SEATS

Valve guides, checking and replacing

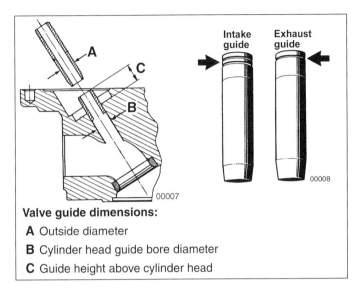

Valve guide dimensions:

A Outside diameter

B Cylinder head guide bore diameter

C Guide height above cylinder head

Service note –

- Use special tool P 206 to check for valve guide wear.
- If valve stem to guide clearance exceeds tolerance, valve guide must be replaced.
- Note distinguishing feature on replacement valve guide (**arrows**): Intake valve guide has an additional groove.
- Ream valve guides to final diameter of 9.00 - 9.015 mm (0.3543 - 0.3549 in).

Valve guide	Outside diameter (A)	Cylinder head bore diameter (B)	Guide height above cylinder head (C)
Standard	13.060 mm (0.5142 in)	13.000 - 13.018 mm (0.5118 - 0.5125 in)	13.2 - 0.3 mm (0.520 - 0.012 in)
Oversize 1	13.260 mm (0.5220 in)	13.200 - 13.218 mm (0.5197 - 0.5204 in)	13.2 - 0.3 mm (0.520 - 0.012 in)

Valve seat dimensions

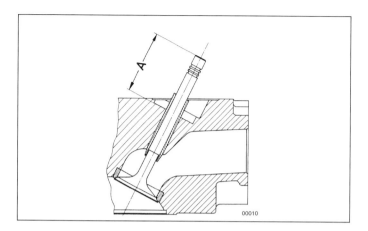

Valve seat height specifications

Valve seat height **A** (use new valve to check;
  remove all shims.) . . . . 45.5 ± 0.3 mm (1.811 ± 0.012 in)
Valve face to valve seat contact area
(Intake or exhaust). . . . . . 1.5 ± 0.1 mm (0.059 ± 0.004 in)

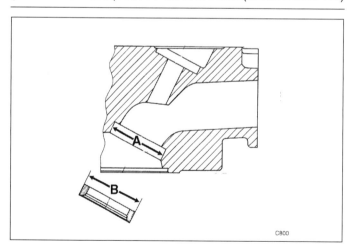

Valve seat to cylinder head clearance

Interference fit
Intake . . . . −0.16 to 0.20 mm (−0.0063 to 0.0079 in)
Exhaust . . . . . .−0.14 to −0.18 mm (−0.0055 to −0.0071 in)

	Valve seat diameter (B)	Cylinder head bore diameter (A)
Standard Intake	51.680 - 51.661 mm (2.0346 - 2.0339 in)	51.500 - 51.530 mm (2.0276 - 2.0287 in)
Exhaust	44.200 - 44.184 mm (1.7402 - 1.7395 in)	44.000 - 44.025 mm (1.7323 - 1.7333 in)
Oversize 1 Intake	52.000 - 51.981 mm (2.0472 - 2.0465 in)	51.820 - 51.850 mm (2.0401 - 2.0413 in)
Exhaust	44.760 - 44.744 mm (1.7622 - 1.7616 in)	44.560 - 44.585 mm (1.7543 - 1.7553 in)

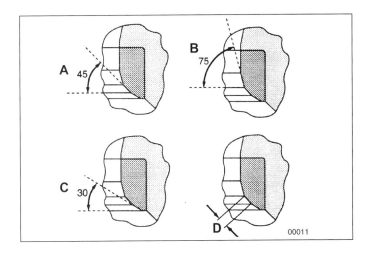

Valve seat angles

Valve seat angle (**A**) . . . . 45°
Valve seat lower edge (**B**) . . . . 75°
Valve seat upper edge (**C**). . . . . 30°
Seat width (**D**)
Intake. . . . . .1.3 ± 0.1 mm (0.051 ± 0.004 in)
Exhaust . . . . .1.5 ± 0.1 mm (0.059 ± 0.004 in)

Valves and valve springs

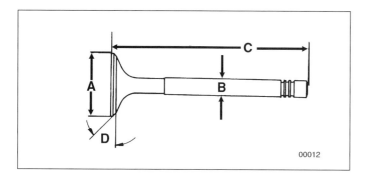

00012

Valve specifications
Valve head diameter (**A**)
  Intake. . . . . 49.00 ± 0.10 mm (1.929 ± 0.004 in)
  Exhaust . . . . 41.5 ± 0.10 mm (1.673 ± 0.004 in)
Valve stem diameter (**B**)
  Intake. . . . . 8.97 ± 0.012 mm (0.3531 ± 0.0005 in)
  Exhaust . . . . 8.95 ± 0.012 mm (0.3524 ± 0.0005 in)
Total valve length (**C**)
  Intake. . . . . 110.1 ± 0.25 mm (4.335 ± 0.010 in)
  Exhaust . . . . 108.4 ± 0.25 mm (4.291 ± 0.010 in)
Valve seat angle (**D**) . . . . .45°

Valve spring height specification (A)
Intake . . . . .34.5 ± 0.3 mm (1.358 - 0.012 in)
Exhaust . . . . .33.5 ± 0.3 mm (1.319 - 0.012 in)

Service note –
• Keep each set of valves, springs, keepers and spring re-
  tainers with corresponding cylinder head.
• Check inner and outer springs for damage.
• Outer valve spring is progressively wound and should be
  installed with tighter coils resting on cylinder head.
• Inner spring can be installed either way.
• Use Porsche special tool P10c or equivalent to measure
  valve spring height (**A**).
• Adjust height by adding or subtracting shims under valve
  spring.

VALVETRAIN

Service note –

- After engine bearing failure, thoroughly flush oil passages in crankcase, crankshaft, cylinder heads, camshaft housings. Also flush entire lubrication system. Remove and clean valvetrain oil supply tubes

Camshaft housing assembly

00028

1. Oil tube plug. Coat with Optimoly®HT, then press in.
2. Camshaft bearing cover. Coat with Loctite®270 when installing.
3. Plug. Coat with Optimoly®HT when installing.
4. Camshaft housing
5. Valvetrain oil supply tube. Clean spray bores. Flush tube thoroughly when installing.Lock pin to locate oil supply tube. Coat with Loctite®270 when installing. Drive in flush or 0.5 mm (0.02 in) below sealing surface
6. Threaded plug
7. O-ring 6.7 x 3.53 mm. Always replace.
8. Plug 4.63 mm. Coat with Loctite®270 when installing

9. Camshaft retainer.
10. Camshaft
11. Rocker shaft retaining Allen head bolt M7. Tighten to 20 Nm (14 ft-lb) while counterholding Allen head nut / bushing (no. 17).
12. Bushing
13. Rocker arm. Check for wear and score marks.
14. Valve adjusting screw.
15. Valve adjusting lock nut M8 x 1
16. Rocker arm shaft
17. Allen head nut/bushing

Valvetrain oil supply tube

Left and right camshaft housings each contain an oil supply tube for valvetrain lubrication.

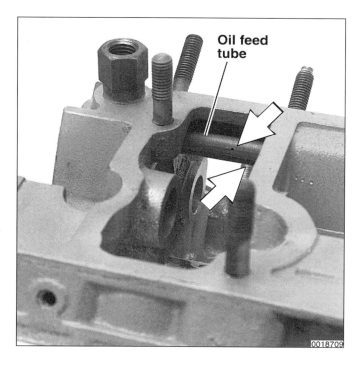

Oil feed tube

Service note –

• On high mileage engines and engines that have had catastrophic bearing failure, remove and clean oil supply tubes prior to engine assembly.
• Clean out oil spray bores (**arrows**) in tubes.
• When installing:
   Orient locating bore for lock pin correctly.
   Point single oil bores up toward intake valve covers.
   Point twin oil bores (not visible in photo) toward camshaft sliding surface.
   Use new end plugs. Coat with Optimoly®HT and press in

Chain and chain housing specifications

Location	Tolerance (B = bore, W = width)	Play	Wear limit
Shaft for chain sprocket mount/chain tensioner housing	B 15.000 - 15.018 mm (0.5906 - 0.5912 in) W 14.973 - 14.984 mm (0.5895 - 0.5899 in)	0.016 - 0.045 mm (0.0006 - 0.0018 in)	Inspect visually
Shaft for chain sprocket mount/chain sprocket mount	B 15.000 - 15.018 mm (05906 - 0.5912 in) W 14.973 - 14.984 mm (0.5895 - 0.5899 in)	0.016 - 0.045 mm (0.0006 - 0.0018 in)	
Chain sprocket mount/ chain sprocket bolt	B 15.000 - 15.018 mm (05906 - 0.5912 in) W 54.971 - 54.990 mm (2.1642 - 2.1650 in)	0.000 - 0.029 mm (0.0000 - 0.0011 in)	
Chain sprocket/ chain sprocket bolt	B 15.032 - 15.050 mm (0.5918 - 0.5925 in) W 14.989 - 15.000 mm (0.5901 - 0.5906 in)	0.032 - 0.610 mm (0.0013 - 0.024 in)	Inspect visually
Bolt/guide rail	B 8.000 - 8.015 mm (0.3150 - 0.3156 in) W 7.886 - 7.895 mm (0.3105 - 0.3108 in)	0.105 - 0.129 mm (0.0041 - 0.0051 in)	
Bolt/chain housing	B 7.857 - 7.872 mm (0.3093 - 0.3099 in) W 7.886 - 7.895 mm (0.3105 - 0.3108 in)	-0.014 to - 0.038 mm (0.00055 - 0.0015 in)	

Camshaft housing/camshaft specifications

Location	Tolerance (B = bore, W = width)	Play	Wear limit
Camshaft bearings	B: 48.967 - 48.992 mm (1.9278 - 1.9288 in)	0.025 to 0.066 mm (0.0009 - 0.0015 in)	0.10 mm (0.004 in)
Camshaft	W: 48.926 - 48.942 mm (1.9262 - 1.9269 in)		
Camshaft axial play		0.150 - 0.200 mm (0.0059 - 0.0079 in)	0.40 mm (0.016 in)
Camshaft/chain sprocket flange	B: 30.000 - 30.013 mm (1.1811 - 1.1816 in) W: 29.979 - 30.000 mm (1.1802 - 1.1811 in)	0.000 - 0.034 mm (0.000 - 0.0013 in)	
Camshaft (runout measured at central bearing, between ends)			max. 0.02 mm (0.0008 in)
Rocker arm shaft/ camshaft housing	B: 18.000 - 18.018 mm (0.7087 - 0.7094 in) W: 17.992 - 18.000 mm (0.7083 - 0.7087 in)	Rocker arm shaft is wedged in place	
Rocker arm/rocker arm shaft	B: 18.016 - 18.027 mm (0.7093 - 0.7097 in) W: 17.992 - 8.000 mm (0.7083 - 0.7087 in)	0.016 - 0.035 mm (0.0059 - 0.0014 in)	0.080 mm (0.0031 in)
Axial play		0.100 - 0.350 mm (0.0079 - 0.0138 in)	0.50 mm (0.02 in)

Camshaft timing chains

Timing chain master link

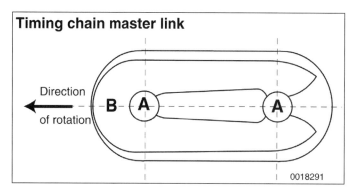

0018291

Original equipment Porsche 911 timing chains are continuous one-piece chains, without master links. Replacing one-piece chain with another of same design requires that engine be removed and completely disassembled and crankcase split.

As an alternative, replacement chains with master links are available from Porsche. The master link makes it possible to replace timing chain with engine installed.

Service note –

• When installing master link:
  -Push in connecting pins (**A**) from back side of chain (flywheel side).
  -Install lock clip (**B**) with closed end pointing in direction of chain rotation.
• Set camshaft timing correctly after timing chain assembly has been disassembled for any reason. Precise setting of camshaft timing results in smooth, vibration-free engine operation.

Camshaft timing

Setting camshaft timing by using crankshaft and camshaft marks gives, at best, approximate results. If timing is not set precisely using a dial indicator, there is a real danger of valve heads contacting piston tops during normal engine operation.

M64/01, M64/02 engine valve overlap

Intake valve opens	4° before TDC
Intake valve closes	56° after BDC
Exhaust valve opens	44° before BDC
Exhaust valve closes	4° after TDC

M30/69 engine valve overlap

Intake valve opens	3° after TDC
Intake valve closes	37° after BDC
Exhaust valve opens	27° before BDC
Exhaust valve closes	5° before TDC

M64/50 engine valve overlap

Intake valve opens	2° before TDC
Intake valve closes	54° after BDC
Exhaust valve opens	43° before BDC
Exhaust valve closes	3° after TDC

Valve overlap adjusting value

M64/01, M64/02. . . . . . . 1.26 ± 0.1 mm (0.050 ± 0.004 in)
M30/69. . . . . 0.60 - 0.65 mm (0.024 - 0.026 in)
M64/50. . . . . 1.05 ± 0.05 mm (0.041 ± 0.002 in)

Timing chain sprocket parallelism

Timing chain sprockets must be aligned parallel to each other to prevent premature wear of timing chain and other components.

Service note –

- If new camshafts or sprockets are installed, check timing chain sprocket parallelism. Use vernier caliper and quality straight edge to check sprocket depth in relation to intermediate shaft.
- If adjustment is needed, add or subtract shims between cam sprockets and camshafts.
- Normally, three spacer shims are under left sprocket hub, 4 shims under right sprocket hub.

Timing chain sprocket parallelism

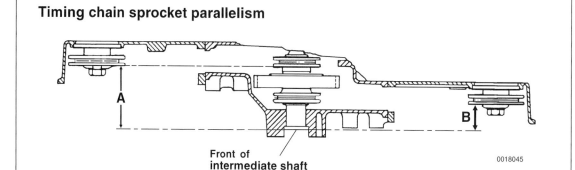

Front of
intermediate shaft

0018045

A Factory distance from end of intermediate shaft to face of cylinder 1 - 3 (left) timing chain sprocket = 98.07 ± 0.25 mm (3.861 ± 0.010 in)

B Factory distance from end of intermediate shaft to face of cylinder 4 - 6 (right) timing chain sprocket = 43.27 ± 0.25 mm (1.704 ± 0.010 in)

17 Lubrication System

17

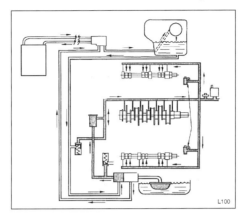

L100

GENERAL

Dry sump lubrication system includes tandem oil pump, oil supply tank, oil cooler, pressure safety system (including oil pressure gauge), oil filter, connecting oil lines.

Main bearings, rod bearings and camshaft bearings are supplied with pressurized oil. Undersides of pistons are cooled by oil spray jets.

Oil feed tubes in camshaft housings supply oil to jets that spray camshaft lobes and rocker arms.

Service note –

- For discussion purposes, crankshaft pulley is front of engine and flywheel is rear of engine.
- If engine is disassembled because of bearing failure, thoroughly flush lubrication system prior to reassembly.
- Porsche engines are equipped with oil pressure warning and oil level warning systems to help prevent engine damage.
- Oil pressure sensor for gauge is located on top rear of engine above flywheel.
- Lubrication system safety features include:
  -Filter bypass to guard against bursting due to over-pressure
  -Four different oil pressure relief valves.

Tightening torques

Oil pressure relief valve caps (M18) . . . . . 60 Nm (44 ft-lb)
Oil tank mount to tank or body (M6) . . . . .10 Nm (7.5 ft-lb)
Oil feed line adapter to case (M24) . . . . . . 90 Nm (66 ft-lb)
Oil gauge sensor to crankcase (M18) . . . . 35 Nm (26 ft-lb)
Oil return line adapter to case (M22). . . . . 70 Nm (52 ft-lb)
Oil drain plug to crankcase (M20) . . . . 70 Nm (52 ft-lb)
Oil pump to crankcase (M8) . . . . 23 Nm (17 ft-lb)
Oil drain plug to oil tank (M20). . . . . 70 Nm (52 ft-lb)
Pressure pump housing to intermediate flange
(use Loctite®270) (M6) . . . . 8 Nm (6 ft-lb)

Oil pressure

If pressure testing shows low oil pressure, one or more of following conditions may be indicated:
• Worn or faulty oil pump assembly
• Worn or faulty engine bearings
• Severe engine wear

Any of these conditions indicates need for major engine repairs.

Service note –

• Make sure oil level is correct before making pressure tests.

Engine oil pressure at 5000 rpm (engine warm)
C2/C4/RS America . . . . .5.0 bar (73 psi)
Turbo 3.3 . . . . .4.5 bar (65 psi)
Turbo 3.6 . . . . .5.0 bar (73 psi)

Lubrication warning system

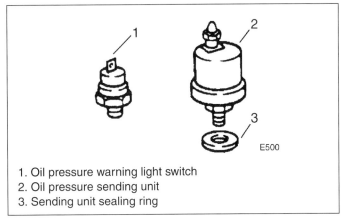

1. Oil pressure warning light switch
2. Oil pressure sending unit
3. Sending unit sealing ring

Lubrication warning system consists of:
• Oil pressure warning light
• Oil pressure gauge
• Oil level gauge
• Engine oil temperature gauge

When ignition is turned on, oil pressure warning light comes on (bulb test). When engine is started and oil pressure rises slightly, oil pressure warning switch contacts open, warning light goes out.

Lubrication system, flushing

Service note –

• After engine bearing failure, thoroughly flush oil passages in crankcase, crankshaft, cylinder heads and camshaft cases. Replace engine oil cooler. It is impossible to remove all metal particles from cooler
• In addition, flush entire lubrication system.

LUBRICATION SYSTEM COMPONENTS

Tandem oil pump

Tandem (dual) oil pump is located in bottom of crankcase. Oil pump removal requires that crankcase halves be separated (engine removed) .

• Main pressure pump (**9**) draws oil from the oil tank and pumps it to main oil circuit and main bearings.
• Scavenge pump (**2**) draws circulated oil from crankcase and delivers it back to oil tank via oil filter.

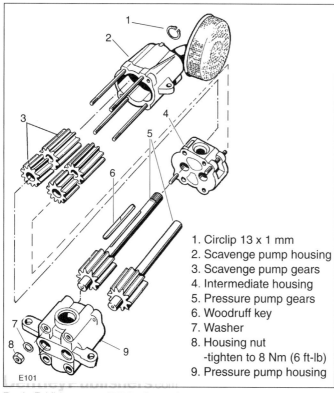

1. Circlip 13 x 1 mm
2. Scavenge pump housing
3. Scavenge pump gears
4. Intermediate housing
5. Pressure pump gears
6. Woodruff key
7. Washer
8. Housing nut
   -tighten to 8 Nm (6 ft-lb)
9. Pressure pump housing

E101

Tightening torque

Pressure pump housing to intermediate housing
use Loctite®270 (M6) .... 8 Nm (6 ft-lb)

Engine oil tank

Engine oil is stored in oil tank in right rear wheel housing.

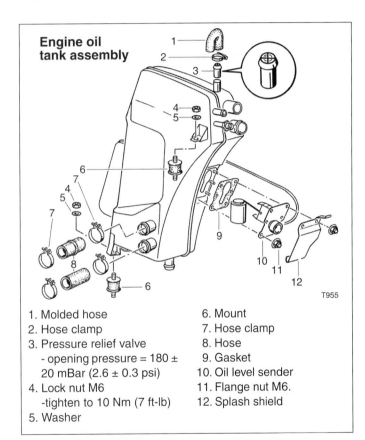

Engine oil tank assembly

1. Molded hose
2. Hose clamp
3. Pressure relief valve
   - opening pressure = 180 ±
   20 mBar (2.6 ± 0.3 psi)
4. Lock nut M6
   -tighten to 10 Nm (7 ft-lb)
5. Washer
6. Mount
7. Hose clamp
8. Hose
9. Gasket
10. Oil level sender
11. Flange nut M6.
12. Splash shield

T955

Service note –

- To access oil level sender, remove right rear wheel.
- Sender operation is similar to level sender in fuel tank.
- Check oil level before testing sender.
- Oil pressure relief valve is pressed into top of oil tank. To remove, pull out with pliers.

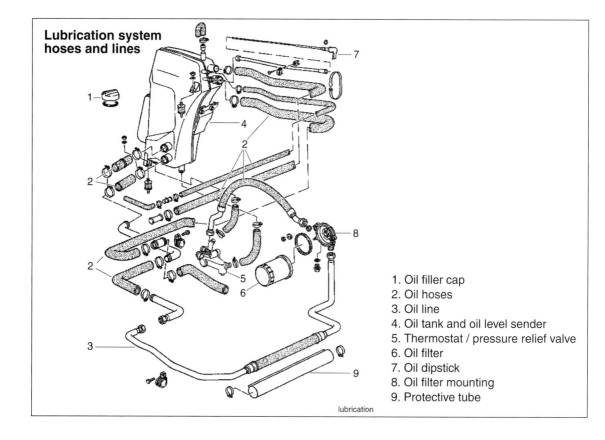

**Lubrication system
hoses and lines**

1. Oil filler cap
2. Oil hoses
3. Oil line
4. Oil tank and oil level sender
5. Thermostat / pressure relief valve
6. Oil filter
7. Oil dipstick
8. Oil filter mounting
9. Protective tube

lubrication

Crankcase oil pressure relief valves

Crankcase incorporates two different oil pressure relief valves. Oil pressure relief valve (**A**) opens and allows oil to pass directly into crankcase when oil pressure exceeds 6.2 ± 0.8 bar. (89.9 ± 11.6 psi).

If oil pressure relief valve doesn't open when oil pressure is excessive, safety relief valve (**B**) will open to prevent damage to oil cooler, oil filter and oil lines. Safety relief valve is calibrated to open at approximately 8.0 bar (116.0 psi).

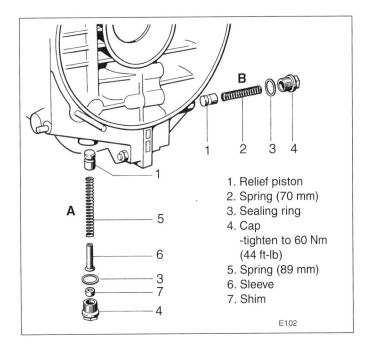

1. Relief piston
2. Spring (70 mm)
3. Sealing ring
4. Cap
   -tighten to 60 Nm
   (44 ft-lb)
5. Spring (89 mm)
6. Sleeve
7. Shim

E102

Oil pressure relief valve spring lengths
Relief valve **A**. . . . . 89 mm (3.504 in)
Relief valve **B**. . . . . 70 mm (2.756 in)

Tightening torque
Oil pressure relief valve caps (M18) . . . . . 60 Nm (44 ft-lb)

Oil cooler thermostat / pressure relief valve

Oil cooler thermostat/pressure relief valve controls oil flow to oil cooler at front of car. Valve is located under car ahead of right rear wheel.

Unit contains two spring-loaded valves (plungers).
- Thermostat valve (**3**), thermostatically controlled, opens to allow pressurized oil to enter front cooler when temperature of returning oil exceeds approximately 83°C (181°F).
- Check ball (**1**), pressure controlled, will open to bypass cooler when oil pressure is excessive.

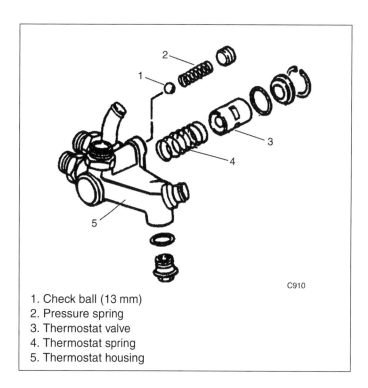

C910

1. Check ball (13 mm)
2. Pressure spring
3. Thermostat valve
4. Thermostat spring
5. Thermostat housing

Oil cooler

Oil cooler is located ahead of right front wheel in wheel housing.

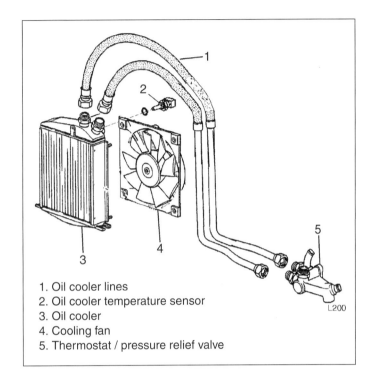

1. Oil cooler lines
2. Oil cooler temperature sensor
3. Oil cooler
4. Cooling fan
5. Thermostat / pressure relief valve

TURBOCHARGER AUXILIARY LUBRICATION SYSTEM

Service note –

• When servicing or replacing turbocharger, pre-lubricate turbocharger with 4 cm³ (0.14 oz) of engine oil before connecting engine oil feed line.

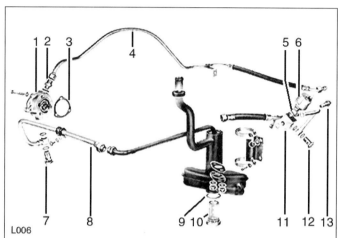

L006

1. Turbocharger oil pump
2. Adapter
3. Oil pump gasket
4. Oil line from pump to engine oil tank
5. Oil pressure sensor sealing washer
6. Oil pressure sending unit
7. Banjo bolt
8. Oil line
9. Oil filter screen sealing ring
10. Oil filter screen
11. Oil pressure sender adapter housing
12. Banjo bolt
13. Adapter bolt

Turbocharger oil pump drive

Service note –

- If servicing or replacing oil pump, see following page for correct drive pin alignment.
- Check air pump drive belt. Replace belt if loose.

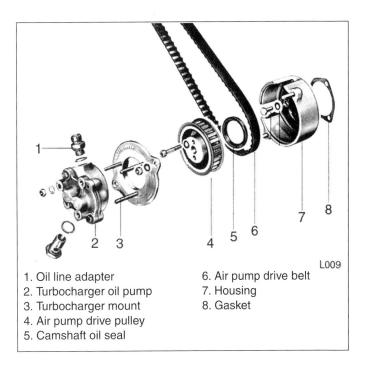

L009

1. Oil line adapter
2. Turbocharger oil pump
3. Turbocharger mount
4. Air pump drive pulley
5. Camshaft oil seal
6. Air pump drive belt
7. Housing
8. Gasket

Oil pump drive pins

Service note –

- Install turbocharger oil pump drive pins to protrude beyond camshaft face (**A**) by 8 mm (0.31 in).
- Position key slots so that oil pump cylindrical pin does not rest in slot.

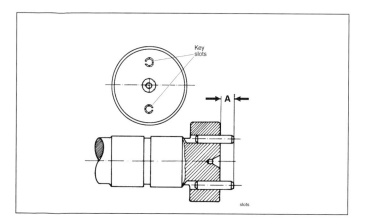

Turbo engine oil pressure light switch

When installing oil line adapter be sure check that ball (**3**) is installed correctly.

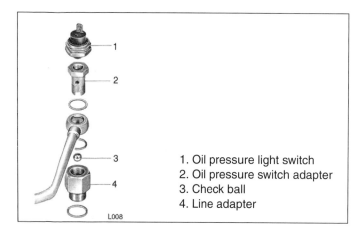

1. Oil pressure light switch
2. Oil pressure switch adapter
3. Check ball
4. Line adapter

20 Fuel Supply

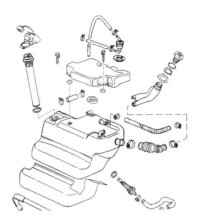

GENERAL

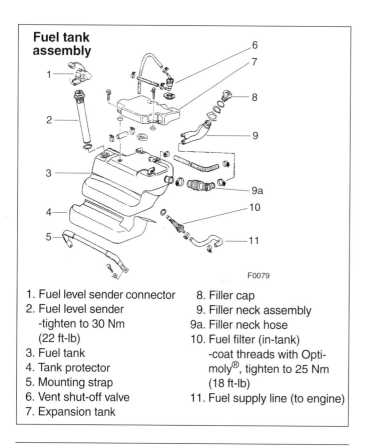

Fuel tank assembly

F0079

1. Fuel level sender connector
2. Fuel level sender
   -tighten to 30 Nm
   (22 ft-lb)
3. Fuel tank
4. Tank protector
5. Mounting strap
6. Vent shut-off valve
7. Expansion tank
8. Filler cap
9. Filler neck assembly
9a. Filler neck hose
10. Fuel filter (in-tank)
    -coat threads with Opti-
    moly®, tighten to 25 Nm
    (18 ft-lb)
11. Fuel supply line (to engine)

Fuel system

Engine management/fuel injection systems
   C2, C4, RS America . . . . Motronic (DME)
   Turbo 3.3, Turbo 3.6 . . . . CIS
Fuel pump applications
   DME fuel injection . . . . 1 electric roller-cell fuel pump
   CIS fuel injection . . . . .2 electric roller-cell pumps
Fuel system components
   Fuel tank . . . . at rear of luggage compartment
   Fuel level sender . . . . mounted through top of tank
   Fuel pump(s) . . . . mounted underneath car
Fuel tank capacity . . . . 20.3 U.S. gallons (77 liters)

Service note –

• On cars built before 07/17/1991, replace filler neck hose
  when replacing fuel tank.

FUEL SUPPLY, DME

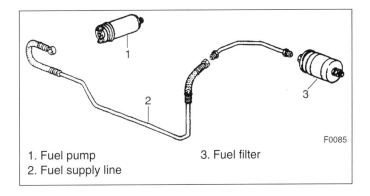

1. Fuel pump
2. Fuel supply line

3. Fuel filter

DME fuel pump specifications

Delivery volume
  pump operated for 30 sec. . . . . . . .min. 0.85 liter (0.9 qt)
System fuel pressure
  engine off, pump running . . . . .3.8 ± 0.2 bar (55 ± 3 psi)
  engine at idle. . . . . 3.3 ± 0.2 bar (48 ± 3 psi)
Residual fuel pressure
after 20 minutes. . . . . .min. 3.0 bar (44 psi)

Main/fuel pump relay, DME

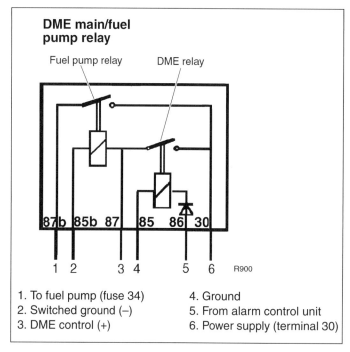

DME main/fuel pump relay

Fuel pump relay   DME relay

87b 85b 87   85 86 30

1 2   3 4   5   6   R900

1. To fuel pump (fuse 34)
2. Switched ground (–)
3. DME control (+)
4. Ground
5. From alarm control unit
6. Power supply (terminal 30)

DME main/fuel pump relay supplies positive battery voltage (via terminal 87) to:
• Fuel injectors
• Engine control module (ECM)
• Idle speed control valve
• Fuel pump relay
• Other DME components

DME main/fuel pump relay is energized (closed) by ECM.

Switched ground to relay is present (terminal 85b) is supplied only if:
• Ignition pulse
• Starter input signal

Alarm system anti-theft protection interrupts power to terminal 86.

Service note –

• When diagnosing no-start condition, check key-on power at terminal 86.

FUEL SUPPLY, CIS

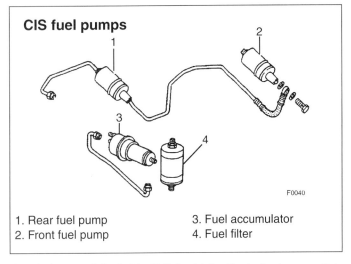

CIS fuel pumps

F0040

1. Rear fuel pump
2. Front fuel pump
3. Fuel accumulator
4. Fuel filter

On Turbo models (with CIS fuel injection), fuel pump **1** is mounted at front suspension subframe. Fuel pump **2** is mounted under left rear of vehicle. Pumps work in series to deliver fuel at high pressure to CIS fuel distributor. Fuel pressure is regulated via line pressure relief valve located in side of fuel distributor.

Service note –

• Add or subtract shims at pressure relief valve to adjust line pressure.
• Adding 0.50 mm (0.02 in) shim will increase system pressure approx. 0.30 bar (4 psi).
• Subtracting 0.50 mm (0.02 in) shim will decrease system pressure approx. 0.30 bar (4 psi).

CIS line (system) pressure

Test range . . . . 6.1 - 6.8 bar (88.5 - 98.6 psi)
Ideal value . . . . 6.3 - 6.5 bar (91.4 - 94.3 psi)

Fuel pump relay, CIS

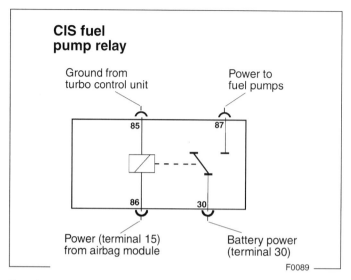

**CIS fuel
pump relay**

Ground from
turbo control unit

Power to
fuel pumps

85

87

86

30

Power (terminal 15)
from airbag module

Battery power
(terminal 30)

F0089

Service note –

- With key OFF, remove fuel pump relay from main fuse panel in luggage compartment. See **90 Electrical**.
- With key ON, check for battery voltage at terminal 30 and terminal 86 in relay socket.
- If any faults are found at terminal 86, check wiring between air bag control unit (terminal 11) and fuel pump relay (terminal 86) with key on.
- Turn ignition OFF and reinstall relay.

21 Turbocharger

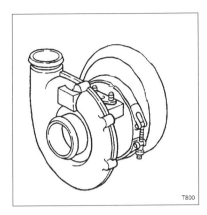

T800

21

GENERAL

Turbocharger has its own lubrication system. Engine oil is drawn into pump on back of left camshaft housing. Oil is then pumped through turbocharger and back to engine oil tank.

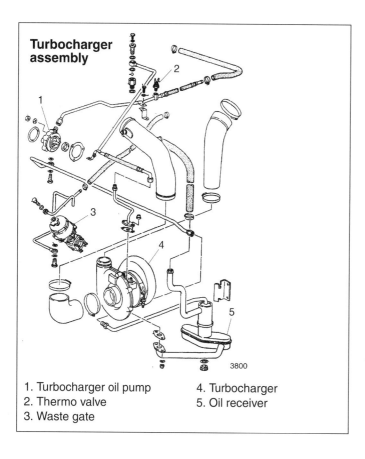

Turbocharger assembly

3800

1. Turbocharger oil pump
2. Thermo valve
3. Waste gate
4. Turbocharger
5. Oil receiver

Turbocharger construction

Kits to recondition turbocharger are available from many aftermarket suppliers.

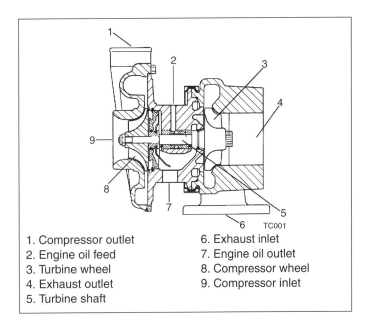

1. Compressor outlet
2. Engine oil feed
3. Turbine wheel
4. Exhaust outlet
5. Turbine shaft

6. Exhaust inlet
7. Engine oil outlet
8. Compressor wheel
9. Compressor inlet

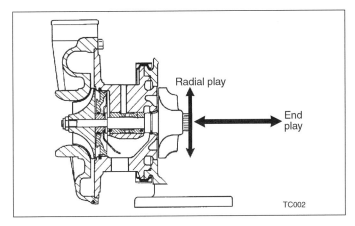

Turbocharger wear limits

Max. radial play . . . . .0.65 mm (0.026 in)
Max. shaft end play . . . . 0.35 mm (0.014 in)

Boost pressure

Test turbocharger boost with vehicle under full acceleration in 1st or 2nd gear, engine operating at 4,500 to 5,550 rpm.

Boost specification
Turbo boost . . . . 0.70 to 0.85 bar (10 to 12 psi)

INTERCOOLER

Turbo intercooler is used to increase density of air charge entering engine.

Boost pressure transmitter sends signal to dash mounted boost gauge.

Boost pressure switch acts as safety valve. When boost pressure rises above set point, switch opens and cuts power to fuel pumps.

Temperature sensor sends signal to oxygen sensor control unit. Oxygen sensor control unit uses this signal to adjust fuel mixture.

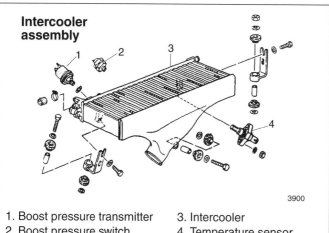

Intercooler assembly

3900

1. Boost pressure transmitter
2. Boost pressure switch
3. Intercooler
4. Temperature sensor

24 DME Fuel Injection

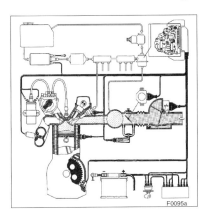

F0095a

24

GENERAL

Carrera 2, Carrera 4 and RS America models are equipped with Digital Motor Electronics (DME or Motronic). DME controls fuel delivery and ignition through electronic control unit (usually referred to as engine control module or ECM).

DME engine control module (ECM)

DME control module is located under left seat.

Self-diagnosis function programmed into ECM software permits faults in fuel injection or ignition to be stored for later retrieval. ECM has permanent battery connection to prevent deletion of stored faults when ignition is turned off. Faults remain stored in memory for at least 50 engine starts.

Fault codes are accessed by Porsche tester 9288 or flash code tester 9268. 1991 and later US models allow use of "Check Engine" light to display fault codes. See **DME Fault Diagnosis (1991-1994 models)**.

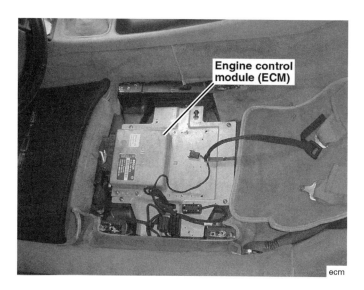

Engine control module (ECM)

ecm

DME functions

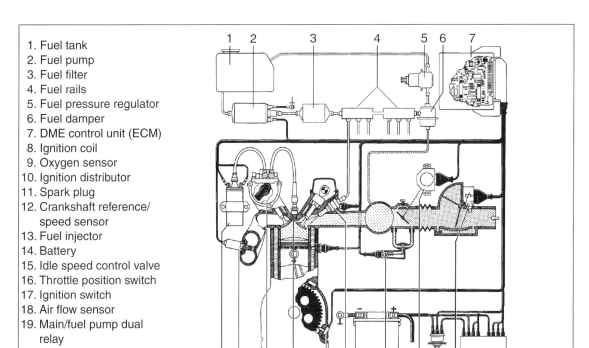

1. Fuel tank
2. Fuel pump
3. Fuel filter
4. Fuel rails
5. Fuel pressure regulator
6. Fuel damper
7. DME control unit (ECM)
8. Ignition coil
9. Oxygen sensor
10. Ignition distributor
11. Spark plug
12. Crankshaft reference/
    speed sensor
13. Fuel injector
14. Battery
15. Idle speed control valve
16. Throttle position switch
17. Ignition switch
18. Air flow sensor
19. Main/fuel pump dual
    relay

DME system main inputs:
• Air flow sensor
• Ambient air and cylinder head
  temperature sensors
• Reference/speed sensor
• Exhaust-mounted oxygen sensor

Ignition timing is electronically controlled by ECM and non-adjustable. Ignition distributors contain no mechanical timing advance components.

Pressurized fuel is injected via electronically controlled solenoid-type fuel injectors. ECM electrically controls opening and closing of injectors.

DME features advanced adaptive control circuitry.

ECM pin assignments

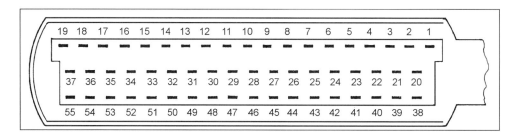

ECM pin assignments

1. Ignition pulse to output stage
2. Ground, output stage shield
3. DME relay ground (fuel pump)
4. Idle speed control
5. Tank venting valve
6. Engine speed to tachometer
7. Air flow sensor signal
8. Hall sensor signal
9. not used
10. Oxygen sensor shield ground
11. Knock sensor 1
12. Air flow sensor power supply
13. Lead L from diagnostic plug
14. Ground
15. ti (injection) signal, cylinder 3
16. ti (injection) signal, cylinder 6
17. ti (injection) signal, cylinder 1
18. Power from battery
19. Ground

20. not used
21. Knock sensor diagnostic plug
22. Check engine control
23. Resonance plate
24. Ground
25. not used
26. Air flow sensor ground
27. not used
28. Oxygen sensor signal
29. Knock sensor 2
30. Knock sensors, Hall sensor shield ground
31. Hall sensor power
32. Fuel consumption gauge
33. ti (injection) signal, cylinder 5
34. ti (injection) signal, cylinder 4
35. ti (injection) signal, cylinder 2
36. not used
37. Power from DME/main relay (with ignition)

38. not used
39. Version coding
40. A/C compressor
41. A/C switch
42. not used
43. not used
44. Intake air temperature
45. Engine temperature
46. Altitude switch
47. Speed/reference sensor power
48. Speed/reference sensor shield
49. not used
50. Heating/A/C
51. not used
52. Throttle valve idle signal
53. Throttle valve full load signal
54. Coding plug, characteristic map
55. Diagnostic plug, lead K

Basic engine settings

Engine emissions

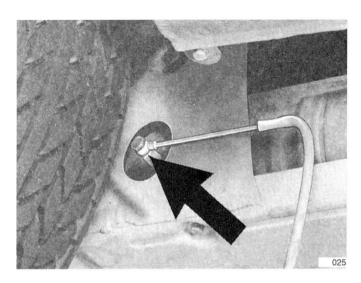

Service note –

- Measure exhaust emissions at idle, oxygen sensor connected. Use test port (**arrow**), at front of catalytic converter.

Idle and emissions specifications

Idle speed . . . . 880 ± 40 rpm
CO at idle . . . . .0.4 - 1.2%
HC at idle. . . . .<300 ppm

Ignition timing

Initial ignition point is determined by crankshaft position during starting, signalled by reference/speed sensor. Once engine is running, ignition point is continually changed based on inputs to ECM.

Reference/speed sensor

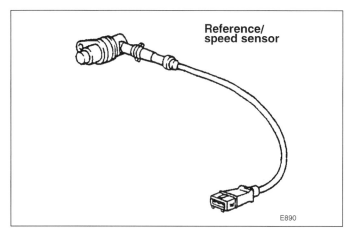

Reference/
speed sensor

E890

Reference/speed sensor mounted to crankcase on flywheel end of engine. ECM needs reference/speed sensor signal for engine to start. Two voltage pulses are generated for each tooth on flywheel.

For more information on reference/speed sensor, see **28 Ignition System.**

Throttle assembly

Throttle applications
1989 - 1990 models. . . . . dual throttle plate assembly
1991 and later models. . . . . single throttle plate assembly

Dual throttle plate models use a small and a large diameter throttle plate. Large plate starts to open after small plate has opened 5°.

Service note –

• Adjust throttle set screw only if factory setting has been tampered with.

Fuel system pressures

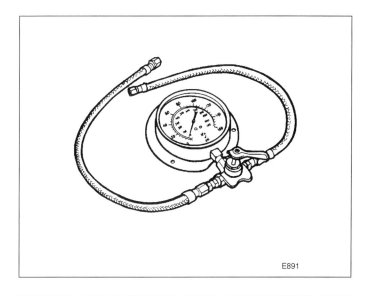

E891

Fuel delivery specifications

Fuel pump delivery rate. . . . . 850 cm³ (29 oz)/30 seconds
Fuel pressure with fuel pump
  relay bridged (bypassed). . . . . . 3.8 ± 0.2 bar (55 ± 3 psi)
Fuel pressure with
  engine running . . . . 3.3 ± 0.2 bar (48 ± 3 psi)
Residual pressure test. . . . . . 3.0 bar (44 psi) after 20 min.

SYSTEM COMPONENTS

Fuel injectors

Injector flow tests require specialized equipment that opens each injector for a precise amount of time to measure fuel delivery.

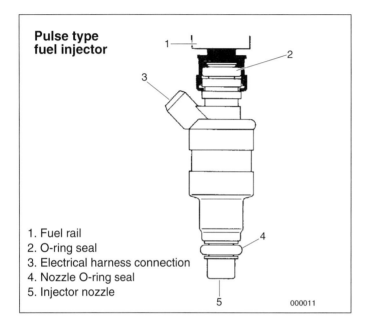

Pulse type fuel injector

1. Fuel rail
2. O-ring seal
3. Electrical harness connection
4. Nozzle O-ring seal
5. Injector nozzle

000011

Service note –

• Injector quick test:
  Start engine and place screwdriver or finger on injector body. Slight vibration or buzzing sound indicates that injector is functioning electrically.

Air flow sensor

Volume of air entering engine is electrically measured by air flow sensor. Sensor-vane is mechanically connected to the potentiometer inside sensor housing. A reference voltage is sent through sensor potentiometer, converted into air volume signal based on position of vane.

Air flow sensor contains integral intake air temperature (IAT) sensor to modify/correct intake air signal from air flow sensor based on intake air temperature.

Correct sensor operation depends on free sensor vane movement.

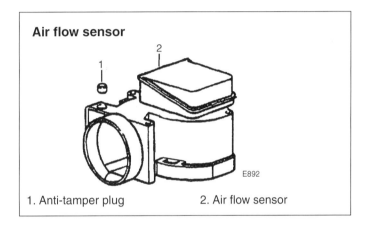

Air flow sensor

E892

1. Anti-tamper plug   2. Air flow sensor

Service note –

- Manually check vane by moving it through full travel range.
- Check that vane returns to closed position smoothly. If vane binds at any point, remove sensor to check for problems. If vane cannot be made to move freely, replace air flow sensor.

Intake air temperature (IAT) sensor

IAT sensor is integrated into air flow sensor housing and is not available separately.

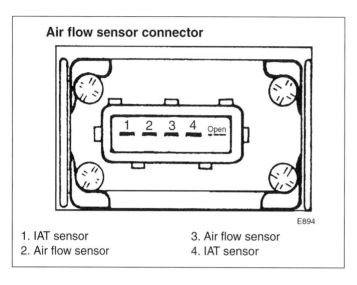

Air flow sensor connector

E894

1. IAT sensor
2. Air flow sensor
3. Air flow sensor
4. IAT sensor

Service note –

• To test IAT sensor:
  -Connect ohmmeter across terminals **1** and **4** of air flow sensor connector.
  -Compare readings to specifications in table below.

Air temperature	Resistance in kΩ
0°C (32°F)	4.4 – 6.8
15° – 30°C (60° – 85°F)	1.4 – 3.6
40°C (105°F)	1.0 – 1.3

Cylinder head temperature sensor

Cylinder head temperature signal is main ECM input.

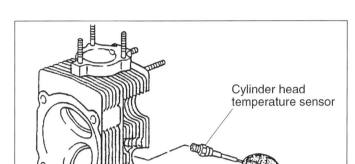

Cylinder head
temperature sensor

E895

Service note –

• Open (break) in cylinder head temperature sensor causes DME system to run rich.
• Short circuit in temperature sensor causes DME system to run lean.
• Cylinder head temperature sensor is in cylinder head 3.

Test temperature	Resistance in kΩ
0°C (32°F)	4.4 – 6.8
15 – 30°C (60 – 85°F)	1.4 – 3.6
40°C (105°F)	1.0 – 1.3
80°C (175°F)	0.250 – 0.390
100°C (212°F)	0.160 – 0.210
130°C (265°F)	0.090

Idle speed control valve

Idle speed control valve regulates volume of air that by-passes throttle to increase or decrease idle speed. Whenever idle position switch is closed, valve is in operation.

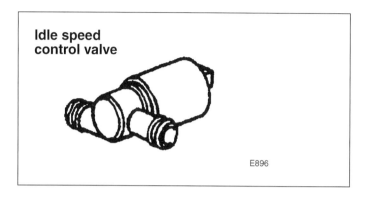

Idle speed control valve

E896

Idle speed control valve quick test
Start engine.
Listen and feel for valve vibration or humming.

Fuel pressure regulator

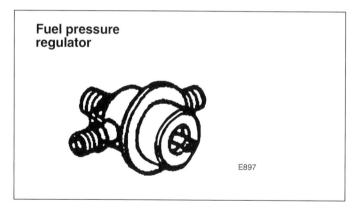

Fuel pressure regulator

E897

Fuel pressure is maintained by fuel pressure regulator. Pressure controlled by spring/vacuum diaphragm inside regulator.

See **Fuel system pressures** earlier in this group.

Throttle position switches

ECM input from two switches on throttle housing:
- Throttle position switch signals closed throttle. This cuts off fuel during deceleration. Injectors are reenergized at 1,080 rpm when coasting, idle speed control valve is activated.
- Microswitch signals fully open throttle. ECM substitutes enrichment fuel delivery from ignition map for optimum power. Oxygen sensor signal is ignored.

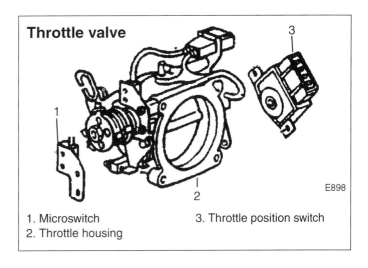

Throttle valve

E898

1. Microswitch
2. Throttle housing

3. Throttle position switch

Altitude correction switch

Altitude correction switch closes at 1,000 meters (3,280 feet) above sea level, leans fuel mixture by 0.5% to 1.0%.

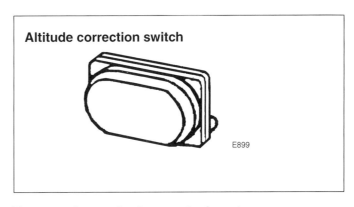

Altitude correction switch

E899

Evaporative emission control system

Charcoal canister collects and stores fuel vapors from the fuel tank when engine idling or stopped. During normal driving, fuel vapors drawn into engine and burned.

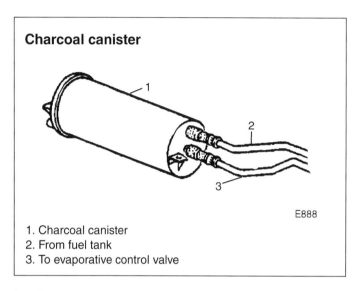

Charcoal canister

E888

1. Charcoal canister
2. From fuel tank
3. To evaporative control valve

Service note –

• Faulty evaporative emission control system can cause hard starting warm, erratic idle, poor acceleration if fuel vapors drawn into engine at wrong time. Restrictor prevents rapid canister purging.

• Faulty evaporative emission control system usually affects driveability only when engine warm and/or outside temperatures high (prolonged idling on a hot day). Evaporative emission system faults not normally cause of cold running problems.

Oxygen sensor system

Oxygen sensor system provides the ECM with information about combustion efficiency. The signal is used to fine tune air-fuel mixture.

The oxygen sensor signal not reliable until sensor reaches operating temperature (approx. 300°C / 572°F). A separate heater circuit assists in bringing oxygen sensor up to operating temperature rapidly after cold start.

The heated oxygen sensor is mounted in inlet end of catalytic converter. Heater circuit gets power from terminal 87b of main/fuel pump relay, protected by fuse 34 in main fuse panel.

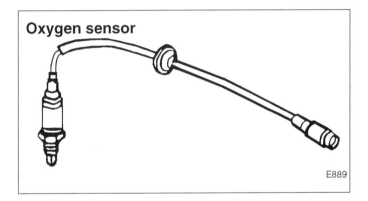

Oxygen sensor

E889

Oxygen sensor voltage output
Engine warm . . . . 0.1 - 0.9 VDC fluctuating

Caution–
- Lubricating sprays containing silicone will damage the oxygen sensor. Handle oxygen sensor with care. Hitting or dropping will damage it.

DME FAULT DIAGNOSIS (1991 - 1994 MODELS)

964s delivered to the USA built after May 1990 (start of US model year 1991) are fitted with a Check Engine light in the instrument cluster.

An illuminated light indicates that an emissions (engine management) fault has been detected and stored in the DME fault memory.

Service note –

• If the Check Engine light is illuminated, faults can be 'read out' by interpreting the flashes or blinks of the light. Depressing the accelerator pedal with engine not running and the ignition on for 3 seconds will start the read out. Consult the **DME fault code table** for code descriptions.

The Bosch 9268 tester or the Bosch 9288 tester can be used to access DME fault memory. The Bosch 9268 is a simple flash (blink) code reader and the Bosch 9288 (also known as the "Hammer") is a more sophisticated tester.

Testers are connected to the 19-pin diagnostic plug in the right footwell. Adapter lead part number 9268/2 is required when using the Bosch 9268 tester. The Bosch 9288 tester plugs directly into the diagnostic plug.

**Bosch 9288 tester
(blink code reader)**

**Bosch 9288 "Hammer"
tester**

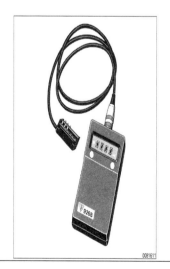

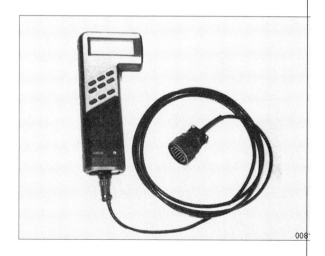

Service note –

- Always connect diagnostic tester with ignition off.
- The Bosch 9288 tester is also capable of reading engine parameter (live) data.

Diagnostic plug location

Behind right side footwell trim

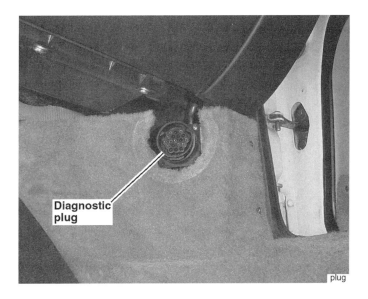

Diagnostic plug

DME fault code table

A listing of fault codes is shown in the table that follows.

Blink Code (Bosch 9268)	Fault description (Bosch 9288 "Hammer")
1500	No fault
1111	Supply voltage failure
1112	Idle speed contact ground short
1115	Idle speed contact break
1113	Full load contact ground short
1114	Engine temperature sensor
1121	Air flow sensor
1122	Idle speed control
1123	Oxygen regulation stop
1124	Oxygen sensor signal failure
1125	Air temperature sensor
1131	Knock sensor I
1132	Knock sensor II
1133	Knock sensor control unit (inside DME)
1134	Hall sensor
1141	Control unit or aftermarket chip installed
1143	Tank venting valve
1144	Resonance plate
1145	Check Engine warning lamp
1151	Injection valve 1
1152	Injection valve 2
1153	Injection valve 3
1154	Injection valve 4
1155	Injection valve 5
1156	Injection valve 6

Blink Code (Bosch 9268)	Fault description (Bosch 9288 "Hammer")
1211	Intermittent supply voltage failure
1212	Intermittent idle speed contact ground short
1215	Intermittent idle speed contact break
1213	Intermittent full load contact ground short
1214	Intermittent engine temperature sensor
1221	Intermittent air flow sensor
1222	Intermittent idle speed control
1223	Intermittent oxygen regulation stop
1224	Intermittent oxygen sensor signal failure
1225	Intermittent air temperature sensor
1231	Intermittent knock sensor I
1232	Intermittent knock sensor II
1233	Intermittent knock sensor control unit
1234	Intermittent Hall sensor
1243	Intermittent tank venting valve
1244	Intermittent resonance plate
1245	Intermittent Check Engine warning lamp
1251	Intermittent injection valve 1
1252	Intermittent injection valve 2
1253	Intermittent injection valve 3
1254	Intermittent injection valve 4
1255	Intermittent injection valve 5
1256	Intermittent injection valve 6

25 CIS Fuel Injection

T9999

Continued on next page

Table of Contents (continued)

GENERAL

Turbo models are equipped with continuous fuel injection system (CIS). Fuel is injected continuously with engine running or cranked by starter.

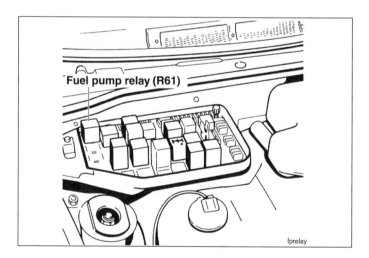

Relay and control unit locations

Component	Location
Fuel pump relay (R61)	Main fuse/relay panel, right rear luggage compartment
Oxygen sensor relay	Fuse/relay carrier, left side engine compartment
Oxygen sensor control unit	Under driver seat
Acceleration enrichment control unit	Under driver seat
Turbocharger control unit	Under passenger seat

CIS hose routing

Use accompanying diagrams to check for vacuum/pressure leaks.

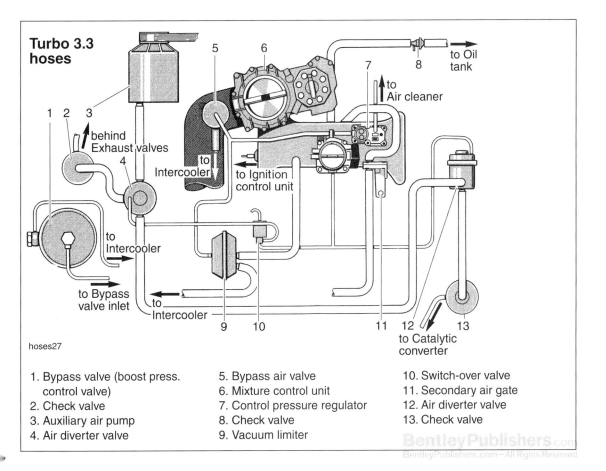

Turbo 3.3 hoses

5
6
7
8   to Oil tank
to Air cleaner
1   2   3
behind Exhaust valves
4
to Intercooler
to Ignition control unit
to Intercooler
to Bypass valve inlet
to Intercooler
9   10   11   12   13
to Catalytic converter

hoses27

1. Bypass valve (boost press. control valve)
2. Check valve
3. Auxiliary air pump
4. Air diverter valve
5. Bypass air valve
6. Mixture control unit
7. Control pressure regulator
8. Check valve
9. Vacuum limiter
10. Switch-over valve
11. Secondary air gate
12. Air diverter valve
13. Check valve

Turbo 3.6 hoses

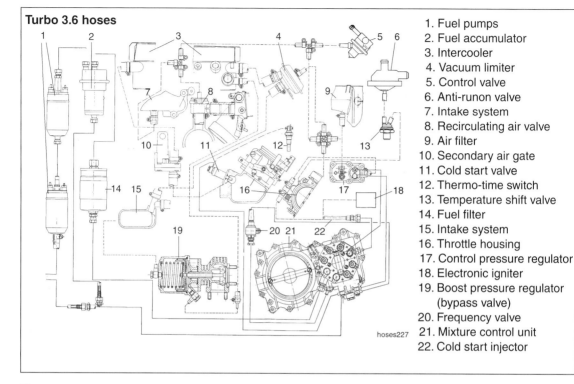

1. Fuel pumps
2. Fuel accumulator
3. Intercooler
4. Vacuum limiter
5. Control valve
6. Anti-runon valve
7. Intake system
8. Recirculating air valve
9. Air filter
10. Secondary air gate
11. Cold start valve
12. Thermo-time switch
13. Temperature shift valve
14. Fuel filter
15. Intake system
16. Throttle housing
17. Control pressure regulator
18. Electronic igniter
19. Boost pressure regulator
    (bypass valve)
20. Frequency valve
21. Mixture control unit
22. Cold start injector

hoses227

BASIC ENGINE SETTINGS

Before beginning diagnosis and troubleshooting of CIS problems, check to make sure all basic settings are correct. Also, check fuel pressure and delivery against specifications, covered later in this group.

Throttle plate basic setting

Throttle plate stop screw provides mechanical stop to prevent throttle plate from contacting throttle housing and causing wear.

Adjust stop screw only if factory setting has been tampered with.

Service note –

• To adjust: Loosen throttle plate adjusting screw locking nut (**arrow**) at left side of throttle housing.

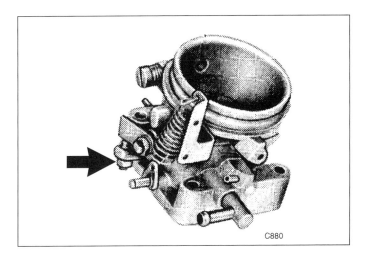

- Turn screw counterclockwise until throttle plate contacts throttle housing.
- Slowly turn screw clockwise until throttle plate no longer contacts throttle housing.
- Tighten locking nut.

Air flow sensor basic setting

Sensor plate and cone-shaped venturi are carefully designed to achieve proper balance of air flow and fuel metering for all flow rates from idle to full throttle. If sensor plate is off-center or binding, or lever has too much resistance, fuel distributor does not respond correctly to incoming air.

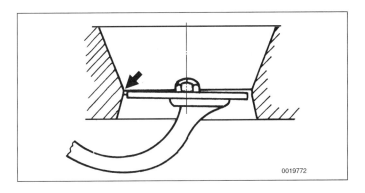

Service note –

- At rest, make sure front edge of sensor plate is aligned with narrowest point in venturi (**arrow**). Adjust plate position if necessary.
- Check to make sure plate moves through full range of movement smoothly.

Tightening torque
- Sensor plate to sensor arm . . . . 5 Nm (4 ft-lb)

Idle basic settings

Carry out idle and mixture adjustments on mechanically sound engine with correctly functioning oxygen sensor system, fuel system and correct fuel pressures.

Idle adjusting pre-conditions:
- Fully warm up engine (oil temperature 85°-95°C / 185°-203°F). This will ensure control pressure regulator is not influencing idle speed.
- Switch off all electrical consumers.
- Carry out adjustments as rapidly as possible to keep intake passages from heating up. This would produce incorrect CO readings.
- Air filter must be installed.
- Disconnect oxygen sensor connector at upper air injection pump mount.
- Disconnect and plug air hose leading from air injection pump to air diverter valve.
- Use appropriate exhaust gas analyzer test equipment.

Idle mixture

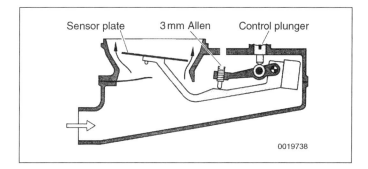

Adjust idle mixture (%CO) with 3 mm Allen wrench.
• Turn screw clockwise to richen mixture.
• Turn screw counterclockwise to lean mixture.

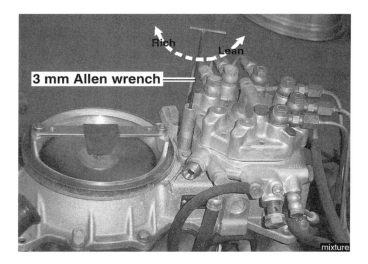

• Adjust mixture with engine not running in order to avoid bending sensor plate arm.
• Make small adjustments. Remove tool before starting engine. Raise engine speed a few times before rechecking mixture.
• When finished, check sensor duty cycle using Bosch Hammer (Porsche tester 9288) at diagnostic plug.

Oxygen sensor
Duty cycle . . . . .20% - 80%

Idle speed

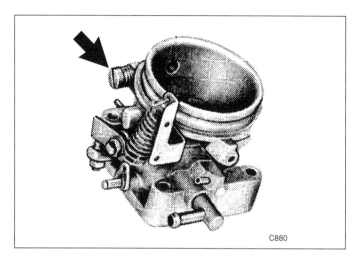

C880

Service note –

• Use air by-pass screw (**arrow**) to set idle speed.

Idle and mixture specifications
Idle mixture (%CO) . . . . 1.0 ± 0.2%
HC . . . .<300 ppm
Idle speed
Turbo 3.3 . . . . 1000 ± 50 rpm
Turbo 3.6 . . . . 950 ± 50 rpm

SYSTEM COMPONENTS

Fuel injectors

CIS mechanical fuel injectors are precision nozzles. With fuel system delivering fuel pressure within normal pressure range, injector nozzles open and continuously deliver atomized fuel into intake ports.

Injector is mounted in insert screwed into intake runner. Injector is held in place by thick sealing O-ring.

Service note –

• In case of hard starting, rough idle, detonation under load, check injectors for low fuel flow or uneven spray pattern.
• Possible causes of poor fuel flow:
  -Crimp in fuel supply or return lines

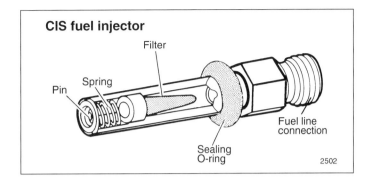

CIS fuel injector

Filter
Spring
Pin
Fuel line connection
Sealing O-ring
2502

-Carbon deposits built up around discharge nozzles
-Contaminated fuel
-Clogged fuel filter

Mixture control unit

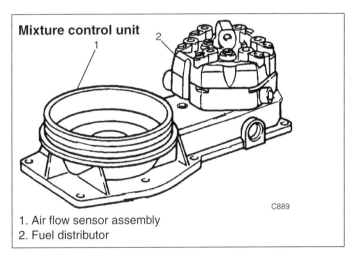

Mixture control unit
1
2

C889

1. Air flow sensor assembly
2. Fuel distributor

Mixture control unit components:
- **Air flow sensor** measures all air being drawn in by engine.
- As air flows past air flow sensor plate, plate is lifted, together with control plunger in **fuel distributor**, to meter fuel.
- Air flow sensor plate basic setting is covered earlier.

Auxiliary air regulator

During cold engine operation, auxiliary air regulator allows additional air flow into intake to raise idle speed. Electrical current warms heating element to gradually close rotary valve and cutting off additional air. Auxiliary air regulator is mounted between cylinders 5 and 6 intake runners.

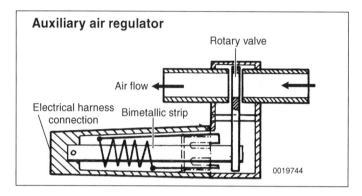

Auxiliary air regulator

Rotary valve

Air flow

Electrical harness connection

Bimetallic strip

0019744

Service note –

- Cold engine test:
  -Disconnect electrical harness connector from auxiliary air regulator.
  -Start engine, pinch off air hose from regulator to intake manifold. Engine should slow down.
- If idle speed does not drop when cold:
  -Remove auxiliary air regulator.
  -Visually check that regulator valve is open.
  -If valve is not open when cold, regulator is faulty.
- Engine idling at operating temperature:
  -With auxiliary air regulator electrical harness connected, pinch off regulator hose.
  -Engine rpm should not change.
- If idle speed drops when engine is warm:
  -Remove harness connector from auxiliary air regulator and check for battery voltage at harness connector.
  -If battery voltage is not present, check for ground at brown wire in connector.
  -Check red/white wire for positive (+) voltage coming from terminal 30 of fuel pump relay.
  -If valve does not close when battery voltage is supplied, regulator is faulty.

Control pressure regulator (warm-up regulator)

Control pressure regulator (also called warm-up regulator) adapts fuel mixture during warm-up phase by adjusting control pressure on top of fuel distributor control plunger.

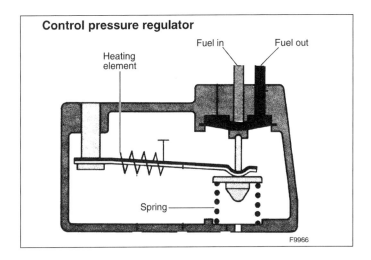

Control pressure regulator

Heating element

Fuel in   Fuel out

Spring

F9966

Service note –

- Control pressure regulator specifications can be found later in this group.
- If control pressure does not increase as engine warms up, regulator is not functioning.
  -Check red/white wire in pressure regulator electrical connector for positive (+) voltage from terminal 30 of fuel pump relay.
  -Check brown wire in connector for ground.
  -If no electrical faults are found, heating element in regulator may be faulty.

Cold start valve

The cold start valve is an electrically operated fuel injector that sprays extra fuel into intake manifold for several seconds when the starter is actuated, if the engine is cold. Valve is controlled by thermo-time switch located in left timing chain housing cover.

When the engine is cold, the thermo-time switch is electrically closed, allowing power to reach cold start valve and open it. When engine is warm, the switch is opened and the cold start valve does not operate.

To limit valve operation and prevent flooding, electrical current heats the switch, opening the circuit after a few seconds.

If the cold start valve fails to inject fuel during cold start, it is difficult or impossible to start engine when cold. If the cold start valve leaks, the engine may receive extra fuel at wrong time and become flooded, especially if the engine is hot.

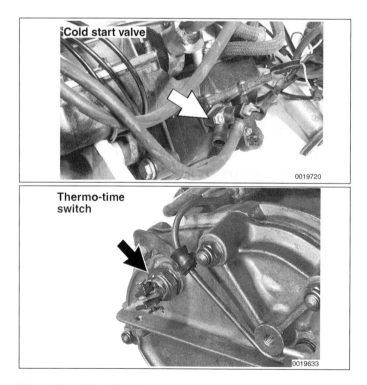

Cold start valve

0019720

Thermo-time switch

0019633

FUEL DELIVERY

Checking fuel delivery is fundamental part of CIS troubleshooting and diagnosis. Fuel pressure directly influences fuel delivery.

- **System pressure** is created by fuel pump and maintained by line pressure regulator.
- **Control pressure** is created by control pressure regulator (warm-up regulator) and affected by restrictions, such as clogged fuel filter.
- **Residual pressure** is maintained in closed system after engine and fuel pump shut off.
- **Delivery volume** is measured at fuel filter outlet.

Fuel pressure, testing

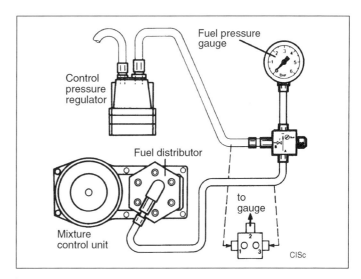

Use accurate fuel pressure gauge with integral 3-way valve to make fuel delivery tests. Install gauge between fuel distributor output and control pressure regulator input.

System pressure

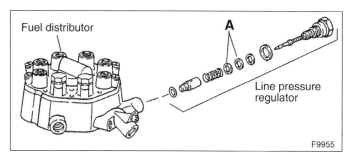

System pressure is created by fuel pump, maintained by line pressure regulator. This is fundamental pressure that all other system functions rely on. Be sure system pressure is correct before diagnostic work is carried out.

Service note –

- Adjust system pressure by adding or subtracting shims (**A**) at line pressure regulator.
- Add 0.50 mm (0.020 in) shim to increase system pressure about 0.30 bar (4 psi).
- Subtract 0.50 mm (0.020 in) shim to decrease system pressure about 0.30 bar (4 psi).

Control pressure

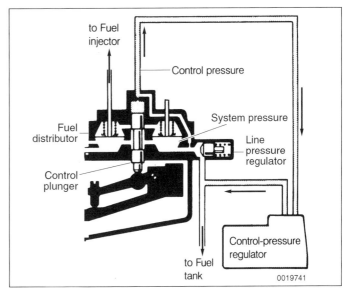

Control fuel pressure, supplied to top of control plunger in fuel distributor, is basis for cold start and warm-up enrichment.

- Engine cold: Control pressure reduces control pressure on top of control plunger for richer mixture.
- Engine warm: Control pressure increases counterpressure on top of control plunger for leaner mixture.

Initial (engine cold) control pressure dependent on ambient temperature.

Service note –

- Test system pressure before checking control pressure.
- In case of cold engine driveability and drive-off hesitation, check cold control pressure.
- Test control pressure on cold engine (below 20°C/68°F). For most accurate test, vehicle should be left to sit overnight.

Residual pressure

Residual pressure maintained in fuel system after engine shut off. This helps prevent vapor lock in fuel lines, provides for faster restarts.

Service note –

• Check residual fuel pressure if engine is difficult to start when hot.

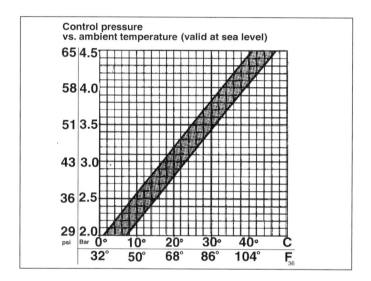

Fuel system specifications

Altitude compensation
   operating range (corresponds to control pressure
   increase of 0.1 bar/1.5 psi) . 965 - 835 mbar (14 - 12 psi)
Control pressure
   circuit fuel supply. . . . . 160 - 240 cc (5.4 - 8.1 oz)
Control pressure
   engine cold and running . . . . See graph
   engine warm . . . . 4.5 ± 0.2 bar (65 ± 3 psi)
Delivery rate,
   both pumps combined. . . . . .min. 1500 cc (51 oz)/30 sec
Fuel injector opening pressure . . 2.7 - 3.8 bar (39 - 55 psi)
Full load enrichment
   via boost pressure. . . . .> 300 mbar (4.4 psi)
   control pressure reduction. . . . 1.1 ± 0.20 bar (16 ± 3 psi)
Residual pressure
   after 10 minutes . . . . .1.6 bar (23 psi)
   after 20 minutes . . . . .1.4 bar (20 psi)
System pressure
check value . . . . 6.1 - 6.8 bar (88 - 98 psi)
adjusted value . . . . 6.3 - 6.5 bar (91 - 94 psi)

OXYGEN SENSOR SYSTEM

Oxygen sensor system provides the oxygen sensor control unit with information about combustion efficiency. Signal is used to continuously vary air-fuel mixture via the frequency valve. Oxygen sensor control unit pin assignments are given at rear of this group.

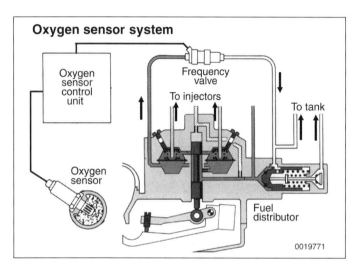

Oxygen sensor

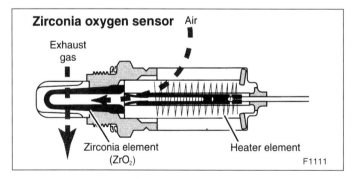

The heated zirconia (ZrO_2) oxygen sensor, fully warmed up, generates 0.1 - 0.9 volt fluctuating current in response to oxygen content in exhaust gas. Fuel mixture is electronically regulated based on the voltage output of the sensor.

Oxygen sensor output is unreliable when cold. Heating element brings sensor element to operating temperature quickly.

Temperature switch (15°C/59°F)

15°C (59°F) temperature switch (**arrow**) mounted in right timing chain housing cover.

0019634

Switch is main temperature input to oxygen sensor control unit.
• When engine is cold, switch open.
• When engine reaches switching temperature, switch closes and provides ground input to control unit.
• System goes into closed loop (feedback) operation.

Temperature switch (35°C/95°F)

35°C (95°F) temperature switch (**arrow**) mounted in crank-case vent cover on rear of engine.

0019632

Switch is part of cold acceleration enrichment system.
- When engine oil temperature below 35°C (95°F), additional enrichment provided briefly (about 2 seconds) when accelerating off idle (approximately 2 - 3° throttle angle) and again at part throttle (approximately 15° throttle angle).
- Switch closed when cold.
- When engine oil temperature reaches switching temperature, switch opens. Acceleration enrichment no longer provided.

Service note –

- To test: Use ohmmeter between switch connector terminal and ground (harness connector disconnected). Test with engine temperature below switching temperature, again with engine temperature above switching temperature.
- For more accurate check, remove switch and test in water bath.

Throttle position switch

Throttle position switch contains two integral microswitches. Microswitch signals are inputs to oxygen sensor control unit.

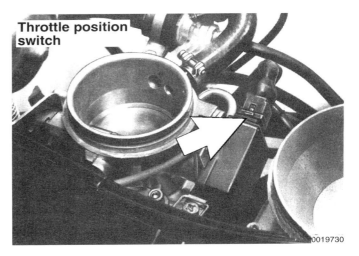

Throttle position switch

- **Idle switch** provides closed throttle input to oxygen sensor control unit. Control unit delays oxygen feedback cycle to prevent erratic idle.
- **Full throttle switch** provides full throttle position signal with throttle from 35° to fully open. Oxygen sensor control unit switches to open-loop, fixed (richer) mixture.

Frequency valve

Electrically actuated frequency valve bleeds off fuel pressure in fuel distributor lower chamber. The longer the valve is held open (higher duty cycle), the lower the pressure in lower chamber. When lower chamber pressure is reduced, fuel flow to injectors is reduced.

Based on output from oxygen sensor, output from oxygen sensor control unit varies frequency valve duty cycle.

Frequency valve

0019729

TROUBLESHOOTING

Test electrical connections:
• Check ground, harness connections.
• Make sure battery is fully charged and in good condition.

If warm idle problems are encountered:
• Check for vacuum leaks.
• Check large intake air boots and intake hoses for cracks or leaks.
• Make sure crankcase and lubrication system are capable of holding a vacuum. Faulty oil tank cap or crankcase vacuum leaks will result in poor idle.

CONTROL MODULE PIN ASSIGNMENTS

Oxygen sensor control module

Pin	Signal	Component	Signal/function
2	input	Oxygen sensor signal	0.1 - 0.9 volts
4	input	Shield	Oxygen sensor shielding
5	Input	Ground	Ground location 22
6	Input	TVS 7°	From 35° engine temperature switch
7		Timing ratio 50°	Activated with throttle fully open
8	Input	Voltage supply	From terminal 15
12	Output	Timing ratio 75°	To acceleration enrichment control unit
14	Output	Output diagnosis	-
15		Timing valve	-
16		Supply voltage	Ignition switch terminal 15

Acceleration enrichment control module

Pin	Signal	Component	Signal/function
1	Input	Supply voltage	Power from ignition switch terminal 15 with switch. Switch ON.
6	Input	Terminal 15a	Starter terminal 15a
7	Input	TVS 7°	-
8	Input	Temperature switch 35°	From 35° engine temperature switch
10		Idle speed circuit	Terminal 5 of throttle switch
11		Timing ratio 50°	-
12		Actuation circulating air valve	-
13	Input	Electronic ground	-
14		Timing ratio 75°	-

Turbocharger control module

Pin	Signal	Component	Signal/function
1	Output	Charge air pressure indication switch	-
2	Output	Signal	Output signal to fuel pump relay
3		Timing ratio 50°	-
4	Input	Terminal 15a	Starter terminal 15a
5	Output	Oxygen sensor heater	-
6	Input	Terminal 30	Battery voltage
7		TVS 7°	-
8	Output	Activate ignition relay	Ignition control unit
10	Input	Terminal 31	Ground
11	Input	Terminal 15	Power from ignition switch in on position
12	Output	Activate fuel pump	Signal to fuel pump relay

26 Exhaust System

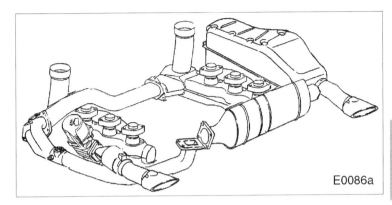

E0086a

EXHAUST SYSTEMS

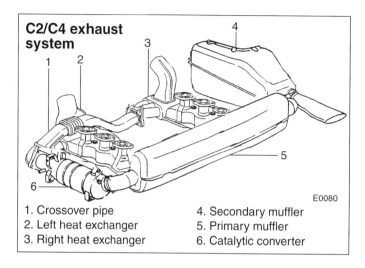

C2/C4 exhaust system

1. Crossover pipe
2. Left heat exchanger
3. Right heat exchanger
4. Secondary muffler
5. Primary muffler
6. Catalytic converter

E0080

Tightening torques, C2/C4 models

Cross-over pipe to
  catalytic converter (M8) . . . . 23 Nm (17 ft-lb)
Exhaust system clamp (M8) . . . . 25 - 30 Nm (18 - 22 ft-lb)
Heat exchanger to cross-over pipe (M8) . . 23 Nm (17 ft-lb)
Heat exchanger to cylinder head (M8) . . . 23 Nm (17 ft-lb)
Heat shield to catalytic converter (M6) . . 10 Nm (7.5 ft-lb)
Muffler support strap bolt (M10) . . . . 40 Nm (30 ft-lb)
Muffler to catalytic converter (M8) . . . . 25 Nm (18 ft-lb)
Oxygen sensor to
catalytic converter (M18) . . . . . . 50 - 60 Nm (37 - 44 ft-lb)

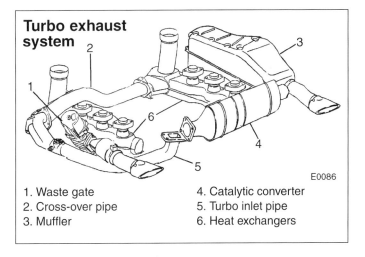

Turbo exhaust system

E0086

1. Waste gate
2. Cross-over pipe
3. Muffler

4. Catalytic converter
5. Turbo inlet pipe
6. Heat exchangers

Tightening torques, Turbo models

Cross-over pipe to
  catalytic converter (M8). . . . . 23 Nm (17 ft-lb)
Exhaust system clamp (M8) . . . . 25 - 30 Nm (18 - 22 ft-lb)
Heat exchanger to cross-over pipe (M8) . . 23 Nm (17 ft-lb)
Heat exchanger to cylinder head (M8) . . . 23 Nm (17 ft-lb)
Heat shield to catalytic converter (M6) . . 10 Nm (7.5 ft-lb)
Muffler to catalytic converter (M8) . . . . 25 Nm (18 ft-lb)
Oxygen sensor to
  catalytic converter (M18). . . . . . 50 - 60 Nm (37 - 44 ft-lb)
Waste gate to cross-over pipe (M8) . . . . . 23 Nm (17 ft-lb)

CATALYTIC CONVERTER

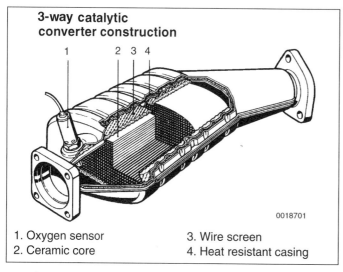

3-way catalytic converter construction

1 2 3 4

0018701

1. Oxygen sensor
2. Ceramic core

3. Wire screen
4. Heat resistant casing

TROUBLESHOOTING

Test for faulty catalytic converter if experiencing:
• Reduced engine power
• Stalling at idle
• Rattles inside exhaust system (not loose heat shields)
• High exhaust emissions measured at tailpipe

Service note –

• Remove muffler. Check for evidence of physical damage inside converter.
• Tap converter with block of wood. If rattling noise is heard from inside, replace converter.
• Test efficiency of catalytic converter:
 -Warm up engine and converter to operating temperature.
 -Measure temperature differential at converter inlet and outlet. If differential is not more than approximately 55°C (130°F), replace converter.

EXHAUST EMISSION CONTROL

Secondary air injection pump

Secondary air pump supplies fresh air to exhaust ports. Oxygen content of fresh air helps raise exhaust gas temperature and lower emissions.

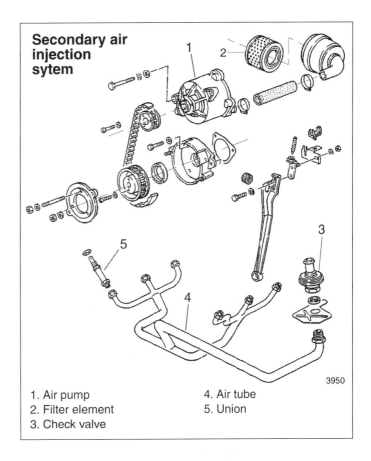

Secondary air injection sytem

3950

1. Air pump
2. Filter element
3. Check valve
4. Air tube
5. Union

Emission air and vacuum system

Diverter valves control flow of air to exhaust ports. When engine is cold, valves are open to increase burning of excess fuel used for cold start and cold running.

Check valve keeps exhaust from flowing back through system.

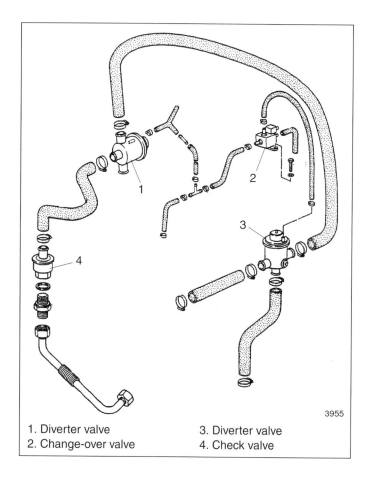

3955

1. Diverter valve	3. Diverter valve
2. Change-over valve	4. Check valve

27 Battery, Starter, Alternator

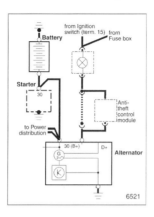

27

GENERAL

Starter and alternator are not protected by fuses. Always disconnect negative (–) battery cable before working on electrical system.

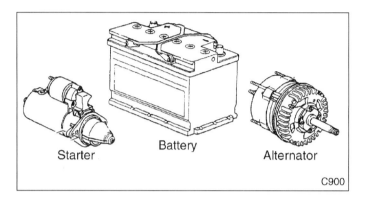

Starter   Battery   Alternator

C900

Tightening torques

Battery hold down bolt (M8). . . . . 23 Nm (17 ft-lb)
Cooling fan to
   alternator (M24). . . . . .14 ± 1 Nm (10 ± 0.7 ft-lb)
Fan belt monitor bracket (M6) . . . . 10 Nm (7.5 ft-lb)
Fan housing clamping bolt. . . . . 8 Nm (6 ft-lb)
Ground strap to
   transmission case (M8) . . . . 23 Nm (17 ft-lb)
Monitor bracket to
   crankcase (M6) . . . . 15 - 20 Nm (11 - 15 ft-lb)
Starter to transmission housing (M10) . . . 40 Nm (30 ft-lb)

BATTERY

Battery, located in luggage compartment behind left headlight, periodically requires distilled water to maintain electrolyte level.

Battery

Type. . . . . 12 volt negative ground
Ampere/hours (Ah) 72

Service note –

- If open-circuit voltage is 12.4 volts or above, but battery still lacks power for starting, perform load voltage test.
- If open-circuit voltage is below 12.4 volts, charge battery and retest. Replace if charge does not reach 75% capacity (see table below).
- Charge battery according to charging table below.

Open circuit voltage and battery charge

Voltage	State of charge
12.6 volts or more	Fully charged
12.4 volts	75% charged
12.2 volts	50% charged
12.0 volts	25% charged
11.7 volts	Fully discharged

Battery charging

Charging rate (low-maintenance battery)	Specific gravity	Approximate charging time
Fast charge: 80% to 90% of battery capacity (Example: 55 to 65 amps for 72 Ah battery)	1.150 or less 1.150 to 1.175 1.175 to 1.200 1.200 to 1.225	1 hour ¾ hour ½ hour ¼ hour
Slow charge: 10% of battery capacity (Example: 7.2 amps for 72 Ah battery)	Above 1.225	Slow charge only to a specific gravity of 1.250 to 1.265

STARTER

Starter and attached solenoid are mounted on side of transmission just above drive axle.

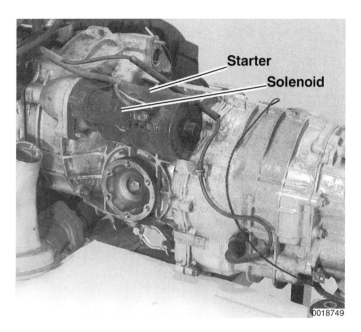

Service note –

- Starting may be affected by engine oil viscosity, especially in cold weather. Be sure correct oil is installed.
- When troubleshooting starter problems, test battery.
- Check battery positive and negative cables for clean, tight connections.
- Check ground cable between body and engine/transmission unit.
- Check electrical connections at starter and solenoid.
- Models with Tiptronic transmission: Check neutral safety switch and connections when experiencing a no start condition.

ALTERNATOR

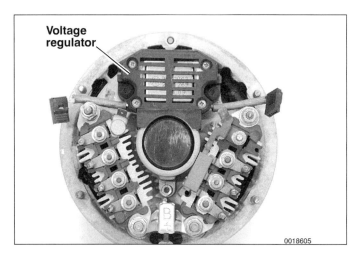

Voltage regulator

0018605

Alternator is mounted to rear of engine cooling fan and is belt driven. Voltage regulator, mounted to back of alternator, also serves as alternator brush holder and is available as a replacement part.

Rated output of alternator (when measured at battery) may be 10 - 15 amps less than specification (see below). Difference is accounted for by electrical consumers.

Alternator output
1989 - 1994 C2/C4/Turbo . . . . .115 amp

Caution–
- Disconnect battery negative (–) cable before disconnecting any wires from rear of alternator. Reconnect battery cable after all wires have been safely disconnected and insulated. (Battery is wired directly to alternator without fuse protection.)
- Never operate engine with battery disconnected.
- Never operate alternator with output terminal (B+ or 30) disconnected and other terminals connected.

Alternator belt and pulley

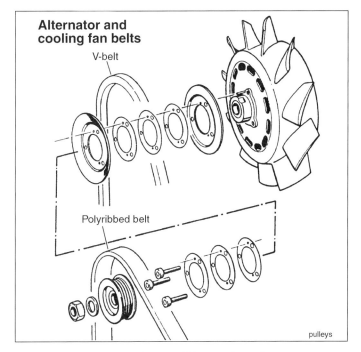

Alternator and cooling fan belts

V-belt

Polyribbed belt

pulleys

Inspect alternator belt for condition and tension.

Correct alternator belt tension:
• V-belt: Add or subtract adjusting shims.
• Polyribbed: Move A/C compressor or pivot belt tensioner.

Note–
• For further details on belts, see **03 Maintenance**.

Charging system troubleshooting

Charging voltage depends on condition and state of charge of battery.

0018606

Charging voltage (engine running)
1989 - 1994 C2/C4/Turbo
(battery good / fully charged) . . . . 13.8 - 14.2 volts

Causes of undercharged battery:
- Simultaneous use of many electrical accessories for long periods of time
- Accessories or lights on with engine stopped
- Frequent long periods of starter usage
- Frequent short-trip driving
- Improper alternator drive belt condition or tension
- Broken or frayed charging system wiring
- Corroded D+, B+ terminals/connectors
- Worn, corroded, or loose battery cable connections

Service note –

- Check charging system warning light for correct operation. Burned out bulb can prevent charging.
- Electrical connections should be clean and tight. Replace hard, cracked wires.
- If tests show alternator and regulator operating correctly, but battery still continually runs down, there may be current drain in electrical system. Note: Clock and some other components require constant current.
- Alternator/regulator quick check: Attach digital voltmeter to negative (–) and positive (+) battery terminals.
  -Make sure tester is connected to clean areas of terminals.
  -Set voltmeter to DCV scale.
  -Start engine and run at about 1,500 rpm with all electrical accessories turned off.
  -Measure voltage at battery.
  -Output higher than 14.2 volts: Most likely faulty voltage regulator.
  Output below 13.5 volts: Alternator/regulator faulty or battery not adequately charged. This may be due to:
    Faulty drive belt
    Faulty voltage regulator
    Faulty alternator
    Faulty battery
- To determine which component is faulty:
  -Visually check alternator drive belt.
  -Keep engine running at about 1,500 rpm and turn on all electrical accessories.
  -Check voltage across battery terminals.
  -Voltage same as before most likely indicates faulty voltage regulator.
  -Voltage lower than before most likely indicates faulty alternator.
- Alternator mechanical noises are usually result of misalignment between drive belt and pulley, loose or broken pulley or worn bearings.

Alternator warning light troubleshooting

Symptom	Test and probable cause	Corrective action
Ignition off, engine off, warning light on	*Test:* Disconnect blue wire (D+) from alternator a. Light goes out: Faulty alternator diodes b. Light does not go out: short to ground in wiring harness or wiring connector	a. Repair or replace alternator. b. Repair or replace faulty wiring.
Ignition on, engine off, warning light off	a. Battery fully discharged b. Bulb burned out *Test:* Disconnect blue wire (D+) from alternator. With battery connected and ignition on, touch blue wire to ground c. Light does not come on: Faulty bulb socket, open circuit between socket and terminal 15 of ignition switch, or open circuit between blue wire (D+) on alternator and instrument cluster d. Light comes on: Loose connection between regulator and alternator or loose connection between brushes and regulator e. Light comes on, no faults with regulator: Internal alternator faults or faulty regulator	a. Charge battery. b. Remove and test bulb. Replace faulty bulb. c. Replace instrument cluster bulb holder. Repair wiring to alternator. d. Inspect brushes. Correct loose connections. e. Repair or replace alternator or voltage regulator.
Engine running at any speed, warning light stays on	a. Loose or broken alternator drive belt *Test:* Disconnect red wire (B+) from alternator. Do not short wire. Using a voltmeter, test between red wire and ground with battery terminal connected b. No voltage to alternator: Open circuit between red wire on alternator and starter or between starter and positive (+) pole c. Exciter diodes burned out d. Faulty regulator or faulty alternator windings e. High voltage drop between red alternator positive (+) wire and starter due to broken, loose, or corroded wires	a. Replace or adjust drive belt. b. Repair wire or connections between alternator and starter. c. Repair or replace alternator. d. Test charging system and replace faulty components as needed. e. Repair wires or connectors.

28 Ignition System

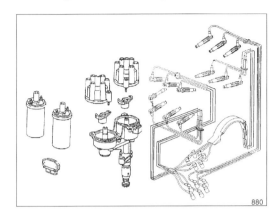

880

GENERAL

Depending on engine application, two different ignition systems are used. Refer to **01 General** for engine application information.

Model	Ignition system
Carrera 2, Carrera 4, RS America	Digital Motor Electronics (DME or Motronic)
Turbo 3.3, Turbo 3.6	Bosch EZ69

For more information on DME ignition system, see **24 DME Fuel Injection**.

Caution–
• Use high impedance digital multimeter for all tests.
• Use LED test light in place of incandescent-type test lamp.

Firing order

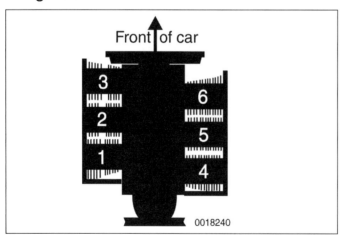

Front of car

0018240

Service note –
• To determine start of firing order, inspect lip of ignition distributor body for cylinder 1 scribe mark.
• Ignition rotor rotates clockwise.
• Cylinder 1 is at left rear when viewing engine from rear.

Ignition firing order
All models 1-6-2-4-3-5

Maintenance

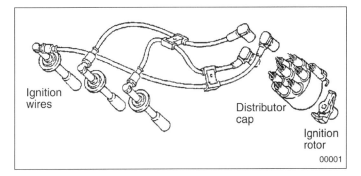

Periodically test and replace the following ignition system components as necessary.

• Spark plugs: Replace every 30,000 miles (50,000 km).
• Distributor cap: Inspect for damage as described later.
• Ignition rotor: Inspect for damage as described later.
• Spark plug wires: Test for insulation brittleness or leakage.

DME IGNITION SYSTEM (C2, C4, RS AMERICA MODELS)

In the DME system, ignition and fuel injection control functions are controlled by single engine control module (ECM). Ignition timing and fuel control are based on engine load, engine speed, engine temperature, intake air temperature, and altitude sensor (barometric pressure) inputs to ECM.

Only function of distributors is to distribute high voltage to individual spark plugs.

Note–
- Models produced after mid-August 1993, distributors are equipped with a ventilation/cooling duct.
- When replacing distributors in car manufactured prior to August 1903, be sure to also retrofit ventilation/cooling duct.

DME ingition components

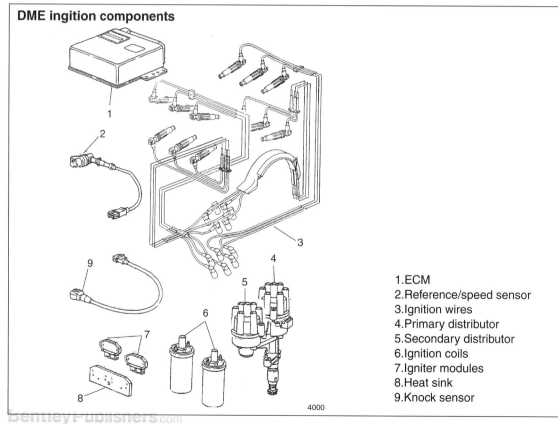

1. ECM
2. Reference/speed sensor
3. Ignition wires
4. Primary distributor
5. Secondary distributor
6. Ignition coils
7. Igniter modules
8. Heat sink
9. Knock sensor

4000

DME ignition timing

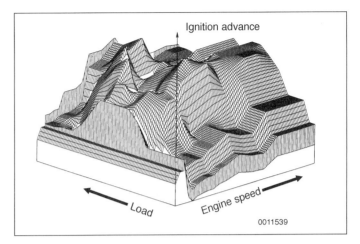

Ignition advance

Load

Engine speed

0011539

In the DME system ignition timing is electronically controlled and not adjustable. Illustration shows DME ignition characteristic map with all the possible ignition points. Map similar to one shown is digitally stored in ECM.

The initial (baseline) ignition point during starting is determined by crankshaft reference/speed sensor. Once engine is running, ignition point continually changes based on various inputs to ECM. Engine speed is monitored by reference/speed sensor.

Service note –
- Use strobe type timing light to test timing.
- Power to light may come from wall plug or from small fuse box in engine compartment left side.
- Attach signal probe to spark plug wire 1 (left rear of engine compartment).

BOSCH EZ69 IGNITION SYSTEM (TURBO 3.3, TURBO 3.6 MODELS)

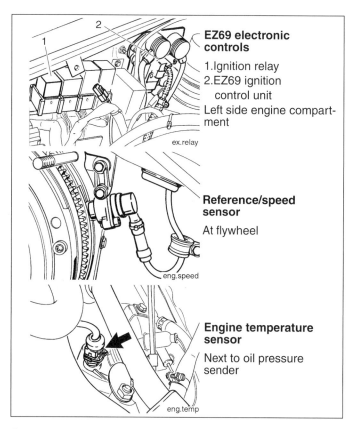

EZ69 electronic controls

1.Ignition relay
2.EZ69 ignition control unit

Left side engine compartment

ex.relay

Reference/speed sensor

At flywheel

eng.speed

Engine temperature sensor

Next to oil pressure sender

eng.temp

Component locations

- Ignition control unit: left side engine compartment.
- Ignition relay: in relay/fuse panel, left side engine compartment.
- Ignition coil: bolted to cooling fan housing.
- Reference/speed sensor: at left of bellhousing next to flywheel.
- Reference/speed sensor 3-pin connector: at left of engine
- Engine temperature sensor in rear of engine next to oil pressure sender.
- Intake air temperature sensor: in intercooler intake.
- Idle speed switch: at throttle housing.

Ignition timing (Bosch EZ69)

Service note –

- Use strobe timing light to check ignition timing at crank-shaft pulley.
- Ignition cannot be adjusted.

Ignition timing specifications (Turbo models)

At 880 rpm. . . . . $0°± 3°$ BTDC

EZ69 ignition control module

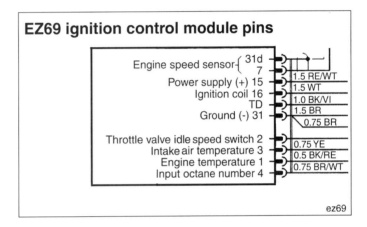

EZ69 ignition control module pins

Engine speed sensor 31d
7   1.5 RE/WT
Power supply (+) 15   1.5 WT
Ignition coil 16   1.0 BK/VI
TD   1.5 BR
Ground (-) 31   0.75 BR

Throttle valve idle speed switch 2   0.75 YE
Intake air temperature 3   0.5 BK/RE
Engine temperature 1   0.75 BR/WT
Input octane number 4

ez69

Service note –

- When replacing module, coat base plate with heat con-ducting paste, Bosch part no. 5 942 860 003.

TROUBLESHOOTING

Warning–

• The ignition system produces high voltages that can be fatal. Avoid contact with exposed terminals and use extreme care when working on a car with the engine running or the ignition switched on.

Ignition system troubleshooting

Symptom	Probable cause	Corrective action
No spark or weak spark observed during spark test	Wet or damp distributor cap and/or spark plug wires	Remove, dry and reinstall cap, wires.
	Faulty wires or connectors (primary circuit)	Inspect, repair wiring as needed.
	Weak or faulty coil	Test, replace as needed.
	Defective spark plug wires	Test, replace as needed.
	Worn or fouled spark plugs	Replace spark plugs.
	Faulty reference/speed sensor	Test, replace as needed.
	Faulty ECM	Test, replace as needed.

Disabling ignition system

Disable ignition system when performing compression test or starter current draw test.

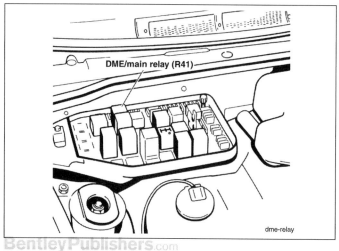

Service note –

- C2/C4/RS America models: Remove DME main relay (R41) in luggage compartment fuse/relay panel.
- Turbo models: Disconnect engine reference/speed sensor 3-pin connector at left of engine.

Ignition coil, testing (DME ignition)

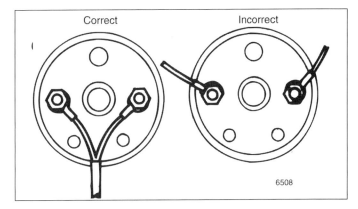

Failed engine control module (ECM) may damage ignition coil. Test ignition coil if ECM is replaced and no-start condition still exists.

Service note –

• Route wiring at top of coil as shown. Loosen nuts and re-position wires if necessary.
• Examine coil for cracks, burns, carbon tracks, leaking fluid.
• Measure coil resistance values with ohmmeter.

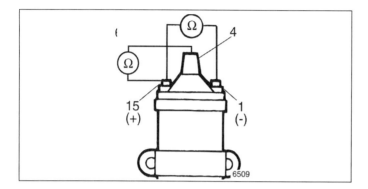

Coil resistance values (DME Ignition)
Primary winding (**1** and **15**) . . . . 0.4 - 0.6 Ω
Secondary winding (**15** and **4**). . . . . 5.0 - 7.2 kΩ

Spark plug wires, ignition rotor, distributor cap, testing (DME ignition)

Service note –

• Check resistance of each spark plug end connector as well as the wire itself. To test connector, use ohmmeter probe on both ends.
• Test shielded ends of coil and spark plug wires at distributor cap and coil using same method.
• Check rotor resistance with ohmmeter.
• Test resistance of cap between tower and matching contact inside cap.

Ignition component resistance specifications (DME ignition)
Center to tip of rotor. . . . . 1 kΩ
Inside contact to cap tower contact . . . . 1 kΩ
Plug connector to distributor cap end . . . . 3 kΩ

Reference/speed sensor location

- Crankshaft reference/speed sensor uses flywheel teeth to determine engine speed and crankshaft position.
- Standard transmission model sensor is on left side of engine at edge of bellhousing.
- Tiptronic model sensor is on right side of engine at edge of bellhousing.
- Access: Remove right rear wheel and detach right heater hose from heat exchanger.

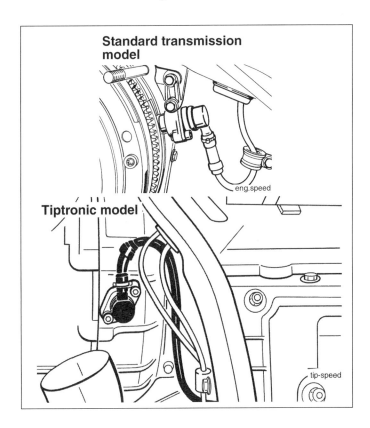

Standard transmission model

eng.speed

Tiptronic model

tip-speed

Reference/speed sensor, testing

Crankshaft reference/speed sensor uses flywheel teeth to determine engine speed and crankshaft position.

Reference/speed sensor terminal resistance

Terminals	Resistance
1 and 2	$960 \pm 96 \; \Omega$
1 and 3	$> 100,000 \; \Omega$
2 and 3	$> 100,000 \; \Omega$

Reference/speed sensor clearance specification

- Sensor tip to
  flywheel teeth (**A**) . . . . 1 ± 0.2 mm (0.04 ± 0.008 in)

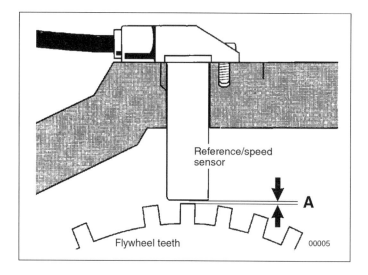

Reference/speed sensor

A

Flywheel teeth

00005

30 Clutch

0018085

30

GENERAL

Double mass flywheel

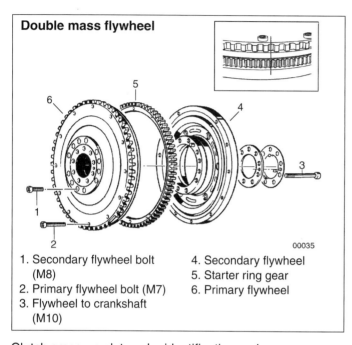

1. Secondary flywheel bolt (M8)
2. Primary flywheel bolt (M7)
3. Flywheel to crankshaft (M10)
4. Secondary flywheel
5. Starter ring gear
6. Primary flywheel

00035

Clutch pressure plate color identification codes:
- C2/C4 . . . . blue
- Turbo 3.6 . . . . red

Tightening torques

Clutch pressure plate to lightweight ("cup")
   flywheel (always replace) . . . . 24 Nm (18 ft-lb)
Flywheel to crankshaft (always replace)
   Single mass (1989 C4) . . . . 90 Nm (66 ft-lb)
   Double mass (1990 on) . . . . 85 Nm (63 ft-lb)
Primary flywheel to
   cover plate (always replace) . . . . 22 Nm (16 ft-lb)
Primary flywheel to
secondary flywheel (always replace) . . . . . 35 Nm (26 ft-lb)

Clutch disc wear limits

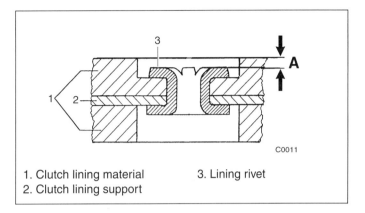

C0011

1. Clutch lining material
2. Clutch lining support
3. Lining rivet

Clutch disc

Lateral runout . . . . max. 0.6 mm (0.024 in)
Lining wear limit, rivet head to
lining face (**A**) . . . . .0.3 mm (0.012 in)

Clutch release bearing

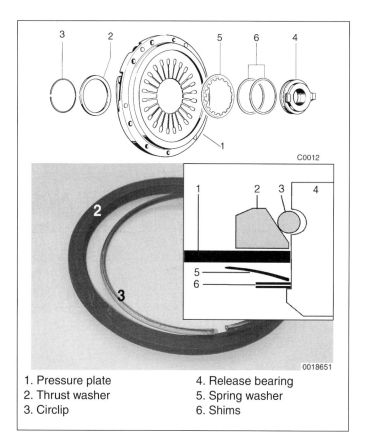

1. Pressure plate
2. Thrust washer
3. Circlip
4. Release bearing
5. Spring washer
6. Shims

Service note –

- Use press to lightly compress pressure plate while installing release bearing.
- Install thrust washer (**2**) with beveled inner edge toward clutch disc.
- Install circlip (**3**) inside thrust washer bevel.
- Be sure locking ring snaps into release bearing groove.
- Number of shims (**6**) to install:
  -C2/C4 models: 2 shims
  -Turbo models: 1 shim

Clutch cross-shaft

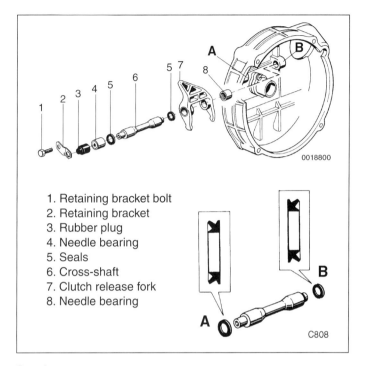

1. Retaining bracket bolt
2. Retaining bracket
3. Rubber plug
4. Needle bearing
5. Seals
6. Cross-shaft
7. Clutch release fork
8. Needle bearing

Service note –

- Cross-shaft needle bearings (**4** and **8**) are not identical. Check proper location before installing.
- Sealing lip of cross-shaft bearing seals (**A** and **B**) must face cross-shaft needle bearings.
- Align rubber plug (**3**) with recess in retaining bracket before tightening bolt.

Tightening torque
Cross-shaft retaining bracket to
transmission case . . . . 9 Nm (80 in-lb)

Clutch linkage lubrication points

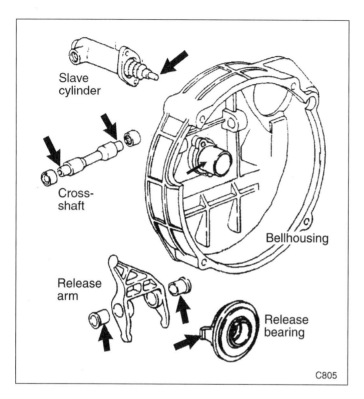

Slave cylinder

Cross-shaft

Bellhousing

Release arm

Release bearing

C805

Service note –

- Lubricate clutch release mechanism surfaces (**arrows**) with Olista® Longtime 3EP or equivalent lubricant.
- Install clutch cross-shaft after engine and transmission are bolted together.

CLUTCH HYDRAULIC SYSTEM

Hydraulic clutch release system is not adjustable. Clutch slave cylinder automatically compensates for normal wear of clutch disc.

Clutch hydraulic system consists of fluid reservoir, master cylinder and slave cylinder. High pressure hydraulic line connects the two cylinders.

Clutch fluid

Clutch hydraulics share common fluid reservoir with brake hydraulics. Hydraulic fluid reservoir is located in luggage compartment.

Hydraulic fluid reservoir

0019082

Fluid specification

Brake/clutch fluid . . . . DOT 4 Plus

Clutch master cylinder

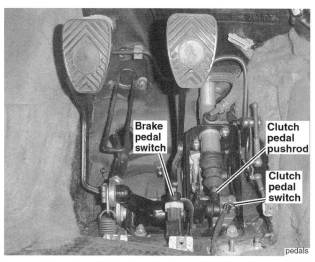

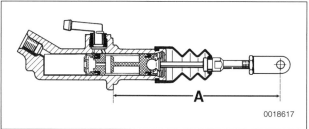

Clutch master cylinder is at clutch pedal linkage, under-neath pedal cluster trim board.

Tightening torques

Hydraulic line fitting to master cylinder . . . 28 Nm (20 ft-lb)
Master cylinder mounting nuts. . . . . 23 Nm (16 ft-lb)

Service note –

• Adjust clutch pedal pushrod basic setting if necessary.

Clutch pedal pushrod basic setting

Master cylinder flange to center of
clevis pin hole (**A**) . . . . 158 ± 1 mm (6.221 ± 0.04 in)

Clutch slave cylinder

Clutch slave cylinder is bolted to upper left (driver side) of clutch bell housing, accessible from underneath car.

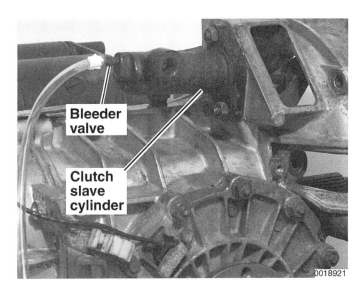

Tightening torques
Hydraulic line fitting to slave cylinder. . . . . 28 Nm (20 ft-lb)
Slave cylinder to transmission . . . . 23 Nm (16 ft-lb)

Note–
• Pressure bleed clutch at slave cylinder whenever bleeding brakes.

CLUTCH PEDAL

Service note –

- To adjust clutch pedal travel:
  - -Detach pushrod from pedal.
  - -Loosen pedal stop fasteners at pedal cluster trim cover and slide stop to change pedal travel.

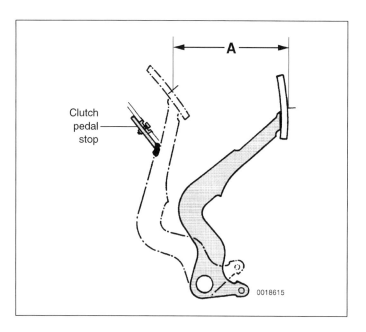

Clutch pedal stop

0018615

Clutch pedal travel

- Pedal at top rest position to pedal at bottom
  of travel (**A**) . . . . .145 mm (5.7 in)

32 Manual Transmission (Rear Wheel Drive)

G50/03, G50/05, G50/52

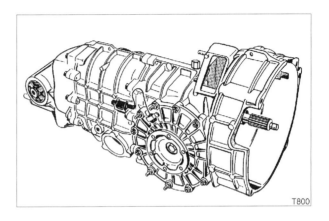

T800

GENERAL

Several different versions of G50 5-speed manual transmission are installed in Carrera 2 (rear wheel drive), RS America, Turbo 3.3 and Turbo 3.6 models.

Transmission number code

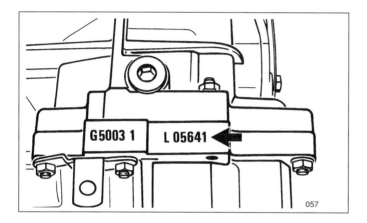

Bottom of transmission case near drain plug (**arrow**)

Example:
- **G5003 1 L 05641**

Explanation of digits and letters:
- **G5003**: Transmission type G50/03
- **1**: Variant: Normal differential
- **L**: Model year 1990 (not used as of 1992)
- 5641st standard transmission installed

Transmission type	Variants	Model year	Serial number
G50/03 (see table)	**1** Normal differential **2** ZF limited slip differential **4** 40% limited slip differential for RS America models	**L** 1990 **M** 1991 (no letter used from model year 1992)	05641

Transmission applications

Year	Model	Type
1990 - 1991	C2	G50/03
1992 - 1994	C2	G50/05
1993 - 1994	RS America	G50/05
1991 - 1994	Turbo	G50/52

Gear ratios

Gear	G50/03 G50/05	G50/52
1st	3.500	3.154
2nd	2.059	1.789
3rd	1.407	1.269
4th	1.086	0.967
5th	0.868	0.756
Reverse	2.857	2.857
Final drive	3.444	

Transmission lubricant

Change transmission and final drive oil every 80,000 km (48,000 miles).

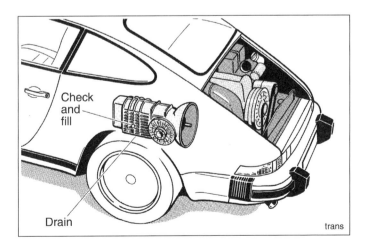

Check and fill

Drain

trans

Manual transmission and final drive oil
Capacity
   Carrera 2 / RS America . . . . .3.6 liters (3.8 qt)
   Turbo . . . . .3.7 liters (3.9 qt)
Oil viscosity specification. . . . . 75 W 90
   Mineral based oil . . . . API classification GL5
   Synthetic oil . . . . MIL-L 2105 B

Tightening torque
Oil drain or filler plug (M22) . . . . 30 Nm (22 ft-lb)

Tightening torques
Back-up light switch to gear housing . . . . . 35 Nm (26 ft-lb)
Breather tube to transmission (M14) . . . . . 35 Nm (26 ft-lb)
Collar nut to driveshaft (M14) . . . . 140 Nm (103 ft-lb)
Collar nut to driveshaft (M30) . . . . 250 Nm (184 ft-lb)
Collar bolt to reverse idler gear II (M8) . . . 35 Nm (26 ft-lb)
Cover to transmission housing (M8) . . . . . 23 Nm (17 ft-lb)
Front cover to gear housing (M8) . . . . 23 Nm (17 ft-lb)
Guide tube to trans. housing (M6) . . . . 10 Nm (7 ft-lb)
Hex head bolt to joint flange (M10) . . . . . . 44 Nm (32 ft-lb)
Hex head nut for gear and transmission housing,
   side cover, tensioner plate (M6) . . . . 10 Nm (7 ft-lb)
Ring gear to diff. (M12/tab washers) . . . 150 Nm (111 ft-lb)
Ring gear to diff. (M12 no tab washers). 200 Nm (147 ft-lb)
Selector gate to tensioning plate (M6). . . . . 10 Nm (7 ft-lb)
Shift fork to selector rod (M8) . . . . 23 Nm (17 ft-lb)
Tensioning plate to front cover (M6) . . . . . . 10 Nm (7 ft-lb)
Tensioning spring to
speedometer sensor (M6) . . . . 10 Nm (7 ft-lb)

TRANSMISSION DISASSEMBLY

Special Porsche service tools are required for transmission disassembly and reassembly.

Service note –

- Match mark direction and order of components such as bearings and sleeves during disassembly.
- Keep each set of synchronizers with corresponding selector sleeve and hub. Do not mix these parts.
- Replace gear pairs in sets.

G50 transmission assembly

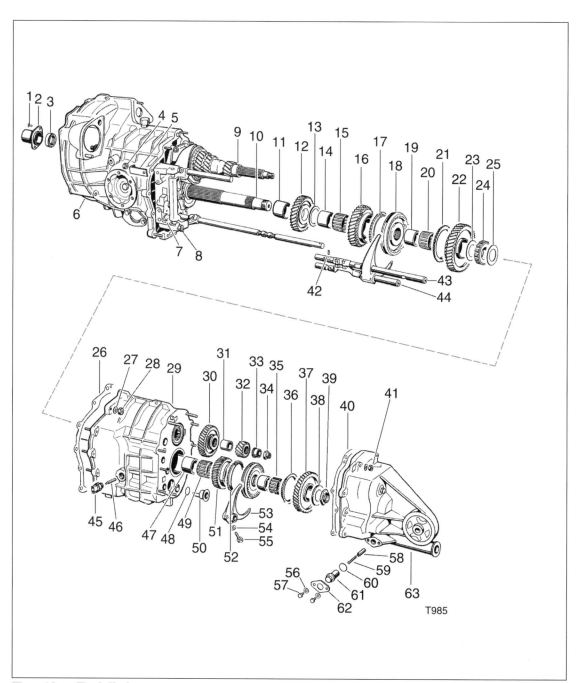

T985

Component list

1. Bolt M6
   - Tighten to 10 Nm (7 ft-lb).
2. Guide tube
3. Oil seal
4. Nut M8.
   - Tighten to 23 Nm (17 ft-lb).
5. Bracket
6. Transmission case
7. Tensioning plate with drive pinion and input shaft
8. Nut M8.
   - Tighten to 23 Nm (17 ft-lb).
9. Input shaft
10. Output shaft
11. Spacer
12. Fixed 3rd gear. Large collar faces thrust washer.
13. 1.4 mm thrust washer
14. Sleeve.
    - Mark before removing with puller. Heat to approx. 120°C (248°F) to reinstall.
15. Needle bearing.
    - Mark before removing.
16. Loose 2nd gear.
17. Synchronizer ring.
    - Reassemble with cogs toward driver dogs (energizers).
18. Guide sleeve with selector sleeve, 1st/2nd synchronizer.
    - Replace with selector fork and rod.
19. Sleeve.
    - Mark before removing with puller.
    - Heat to approx. 120°C (248°F) to reinstall.
20. Needle bearing.
    - Mark before removing.
21. Synchronizer ring.
    - Reassemble with cogs toward driver dogs (energizers).
22. 1st gear.
23. 2.8 mm thrust washer

24. Roller bearing.
    - Remove with puller.
    - Heat to approx. 120°C (248°F) to reinstall.
25. 2.8 mm thrust washer
26. Gasket
27. Washer
28. Nut M8.
    - Tighten to 23 Nm (17 ft-lb).
29. Gear housing
30. Fixed 5th gear.
31. Spacer
32. Fixed reverse gear
33. Bearing inner race.
    - Remove with puller. Heat to approx. 120°C (248°F) to reinstall.
34. Collar lock nut.
    - Lock input shaft with Porsche special tool 9263 and engage 5th gear to remove and install.
    - Tighten to 140 Nm (103 ft-lb).
    - Punch collar to lock.
35. Needle bearing
36. Synchronizer ring.
    - Reassemble with cogs toward driver dogs (energizers).
37. Loose reverse gear.
38. Thrust washer
39. Collar lock nut.
    - Remove/install: Lock input shaft with Porsche special tool 9263, engage 5th gear.
    - Tighten to 250 Nm (183 ft-lb).
    - Punch collar to lock.
40. Gasket
41. Nut M8. Tighten to 23 Nm (17 ft-lb).
42. Locking dowel.
43. 5th/reverse gear selector rod
44. Selector fork with selector rod.
    - Place selector rod in neutral, remove together with selector sleeve and guide sleeve.

45. Back-up light switch.
    - Tighten to 35 Nm (26 ft-lb).
46. Plunger.
    - Stepped end faces switch.
47. Sleeve.
    - Mark before removing.
    - Heat to approx. 120°C (248°F) to reinstall.
48. Sealing O-ring
49. Needle bearing.
    - Mark before removing.
50. Oil delivery tube
51. Loose 5th gear.
52. Guide sleeve with selector sleeve and Synchronizer ring.
    - Mark before removing.
    - Selector sleeve and guide sleeve matched.
53. Selector fork.
    - Remove together with selector sleeve and guide sleeve.
54. Washer
55. Bolt M8.
    - Tighten to 23 Nm (17 ft-lb).
56. Washer
57. Bolt M6.
    - Tighten to 10 Nm (7 ft-lb)
58. Locking bushing
59. Spring
60. Sealing O-ring
61. Eccentric bushing
62. Clamping plate
63. Front transmission cover

Input shaft

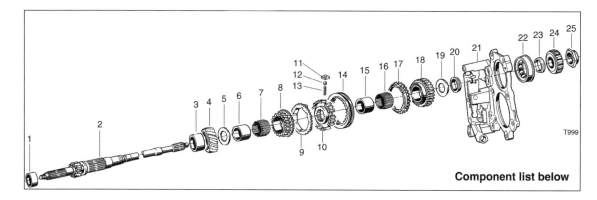

T999

Component list below

Component list

1. Bearing inner race
   - Press to remove.
   - Heat to approx. 120°C (248°F) to reinstall.
2. Input shaft
3. Spacer
4. Fixed 2nd gear
   - Collar faces spacer.
5. 1.85 mm thrust washer
6. Bearing inner race
   - Heat to approx. 120°C (248°F) to reinstall.
7. Needle bearing
   - Mark before removing.
8. Loose 3rd gear.
9. Synchronizer ring
   - Mark before removing.
   - Reassemble with cogs toward driver dogs (energizers).
10. Guide sleeve
    - Remove with selector sleeve.
    - Install with selector sleeve and synchronizer parts.
11. Driver dog
    - Install with domed side facing selector sleeve.

12. Ball
13. Spring
    - Length: 11.8 + 0.3 mm (0.47 + 0.012 in). Thickness: 0.8 mm (0.03 in).
14. 3rd/4th gear selector sleeve
    - Mark before removing.
    - Replace with synchronizer parts.
15. Inner race
16. Needle bearing
    - Mark before removing.
17. Synchronizer ring
    - Mark before removing.
    - Reassemble with cogs toward driver dogs (energizers).
18. Loose 4th gear
19. Thrust washer. Flat side faces needle bearing.
20. Bearing inner race
    - Press to remove.
    - Heat to approx. 120°C (248°F) to reinstall.
21. Tensioning plate
    - Reassembly: Mount in soft-jawed vice. Engage 5th gear, insert input shaft in selector rod/fork with dowels in place.

22. 4-point bearing
23. Bearing inner race
    - Press to remove.
    - Heat to approx. 120°C (248°F) to reinstall.
24. Roller bearing
    - Press to remove.
    - Heat to approx. 120°C (248°F) to reinstall.
25. Collar nut
    - Remove/install with special tools 9177 and 9105.
    - Tighten to 250 Nm (183 ft-lb).
    - Punch collar to lock.

Output shaft

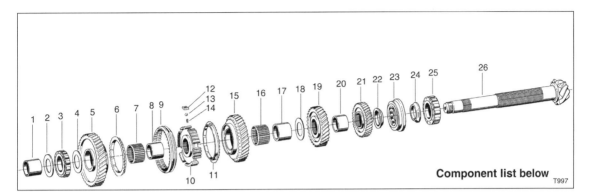

Component list below   T997

Component list

1. Inner race
   - Mark before removing.
   - Heat to approx. 120°C (248°F) to reinstall.
2. 2.8 mm thrust washer
3. Roller bearing
   - Heat to approx. 120°C (248°F) to reinstall.
4. 2.8 mm thrust washer
5. Loose 1st gear
6. Synchronizer ring
   - Mark before removing.
   - Reassemble with cogs toward driver dogs (energizers).
7. Needle bearing
   - Mark before removing.
8. Inner race
   - Mark before removing
9. 1st/2nd gear selector sleeve.
   - Replace with synchronizer parts.
10. Guide sleeve
    - Remove with selector sleeve. Install with selector sleeve and synchronizer parts.

11. Synchronizer ring
    - Mark before removing.
    - Reassemble with cogs toward driver dogs (energizers).
12. Driver dog with guide nose
    - Do not confuse with dog for 3rd/5th/reverse gears.
13. Ball
14. Spring
    - Mark before removing.
    Length: 10.7 ± 0.2 mm (0.42 ± 0.008 in).
    Thickness: 0.9 mm (0.035 in)
15. Loose 2nd gear
16. Needle bearing
    - Mark before removing.
17. Inner race
    - Mark before removing.
18. 1.4 mm thrust washer
19. Fixed 3rd gear
    - Reassemble with larger collar facing thrust washer.
20. Spacer
21. Fixed 4th gear
    - Reassembly: Larger collar faces 4-point bearing (#23).

22. Bearing inner race
    - Mark before removing. Do not confuse with inner race #24. Heat to approx. 120°C (248°F) to reinstall.
23. 4-point bearing
24. Bearing inner race
    - Mark before removing. Press to remove. Do not confuse with inner race #22. Heat to approx. 120°C (248°F) to reinstall.
25. Roller bearing
    - Press to remove. Heat to approx. 120°C (248°F) to reinstall.
26. Output shaft and drive pinion. Match/readjust to differential ring gear.

TRANSMISSION COMPONENTS

Selector sleeve assembly

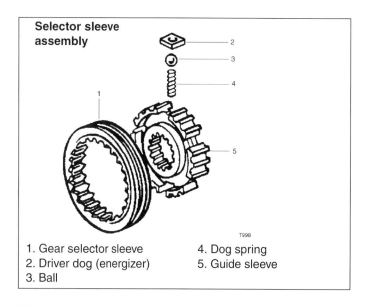

Selector sleeve assembly

1. Gear selector sleeve
2. Driver dog (energizer)
3. Ball
4. Dog spring
5. Guide sleeve

Dog springs

Length
   1st/2nd gear spring . . . . . 10.7± 0.2 mm (0.42 ± 0.008 in)
   3rd/4th gear spring . . . . 11.8 + 0.3 mm (0.47 + 0.008 in)
Thickness
1st/2nd gear spring . . . . .0.9 mm (0.035 in)
3rd/4th gear spring . . . . .0.8 mm (0.03 in)

Synchronizer wear

Inspect synchronizer rings for wear.

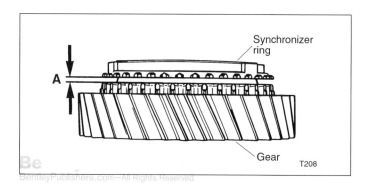

Synchronizer ring

A

Gear

Service note –

• Press ring into gear wheel cone and measure gap **A**.

Synchronizer specifications

New synchronizer
  Gap **A** for 1st/2nd gears . . . . .min. 1.1 mm (0.04 in)
  Gap **A** for 3rd/4th gears. . . . . .min. 0.9 mm (0.035 in)
Wear limit
Gap **A** . . . . 0.6 - 0.7 mm (0.024 - 0.028 in)

Selector sleeve spacing

Service note –

• When adjusting selector sleeve, be sure spacing for **A** and **B** are same.

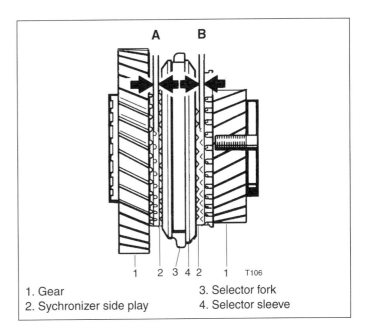

1. Gear
2. Sychronizer side play
3. Selector fork
4. Selector sleeve

Pinion bearing

Large inner pinion bearing race (**A**) must face pinion gear end of output shaft. Small inner pinion bearing race (**B**) must face 4th gear. Heat all bearings and bearing inner races to 120° C (248° F) before pressing on shaft.

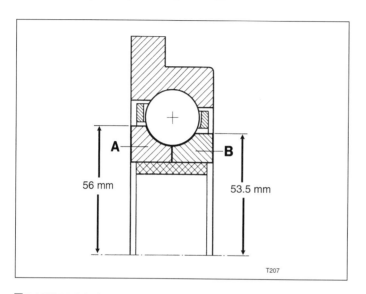

56 mm

53.5 mm

T207

TRANSMISSION MOUNT

Service note –

• Install mount with notch (**arrow**) pointing down.

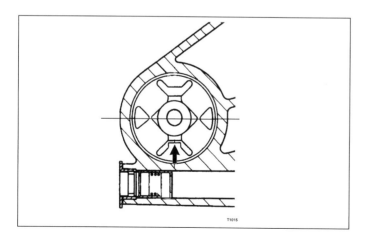

T1015

34 Manual Transmission (All Wheel Drive)

G64/00

34

GENERAL

G64 5-speed manual transmission is installed in Carrera 4 (all wheel drive).

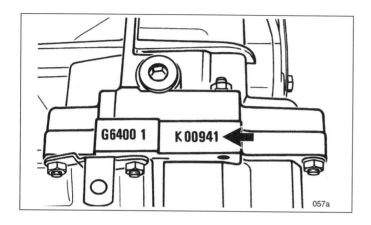

Transmission number code

Bottom of transmission case near drain plug (**arrow**)

Example:
• **G6400 1 K 00941**

Explanation of digits and letters:
• **G6400**: Transmission type G64/00
• **1**: Variant: Normal differential
• **K**: Model year 1989 (not used as of 1992)
• 941st standard transmission installed

Transmission type	Variants	Model year	Serial number
G64/00	1 Normal differential 3 Hydraulically controlled limited slip differential (PSD)	**K** 1989 **L** 1990 **M** 1991 (no letter used from model year 1992)	00941

Gear ratios

Gear	G64/00
1st	3.500
2nd	2.118
3rd	1.444
4th	1.086
5th	0.868
Reverse	2.857
Final drive	3.444

Transmission lubricant

Change transmission and final drive oil every 80,000 km (48,000 miles).

Manual transmission and final drive oil
Capacity . . . . .3.8 liters (4.0 qt)
Oil viscosity specification. 75 W 90
Mineral based oil . . . . API classification GL5
Synthetic oil. . . . . MIL-L 2105 B

Tightening torque
Oil drain or filler plug (M22) . . . . 30 Nm (22 ft-lb)

TRANSMISSION DISASSEMBLY

Special Porsche service tools are required for transmission disassembly and reassembly.

Service note –

- Match-mark direction and order of components such as bearings and sleeves before disassembly.
- Keep each set of synchronizers with corresponding selector sleeve and hub. Do not mix these parts.
- Replace gear pairs in sets.
- Stake collar nuts after tightening.

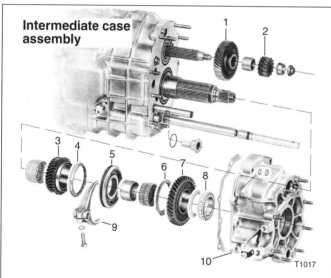

Intermediate case assembly

T1017

1. Fixed 5th gear
2. Fixed reverse gear
3. Loose 5th gear
4. Synchronizer ring
5. 5th/reverse guide sleeve
   with selector sleeve
6. Synchronizer ring
7. Loose reverse gear
8. Roller bearing
9. Shift fork
10. Intermediate case

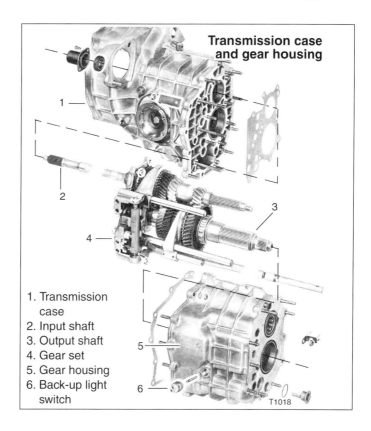

Transmission case and gear housing

1. Transmission case
2. Input shaft
3. Output shaft
4. Gear set
5. Gear housing
6. Back-up light switch

T1018

Tightening torques

Back-up light switch to gear housing . . . . . 35 Nm (26 ft-lb)
Bleeder in transmission case (M14) . . . . . 35 Nm (26 ft-lb)
Clamp plate to transfer case (M6) . . . . . . .10 Nm (7.5 ft-lb)
Collar nut to input shaft (M14) . . . . 140 Nm (103 ft-lb)
Collar nut to input shaft (M30) . . . . 250 Nm (185 ft-lb)
Collar bolt to reverse idler gear fork
  (M8) (use Loctite®) . . . . 35 Nm (26 ft-lb)
Cover to differential housing (M6) . . . . . . 15 Nm (11 ft-lb)
Drive axle to output flange (M10) . . . . 44 Nm (32 ft-lb)
Guide tube to transmission case (M6). . . .10 Nm (7.5 ft-lb)
Lock nut to drive carrier (M24) . . . . 240 Nm (177 ft-lb)
Lock nut to drive pinion (M40) . . . . 240 Nm (177 ft-lb)
Lock nut to drive carrier (M42) . . . . 300 Nm (221 ft-lb)
Mating bearing screw to engaging fork,
transverse lock (M12) . . . . 65 Nm (48 ft-lb)

Tightening torques (continued)

Ring gear to differential
(M12 with tab washer) . . . . 150 Nm (111 ft-lb)

Ring gear to differential
(M12 without tab washer) . . . . 200 Nm (147 ft-lb)

Shift fork to selector shaft (M8) . . . . 23 Nm (17 ft-lb)

Shift gate to tensioner plate (M6) . . . . 10 Nm (7.5 ft-lb)

Side cover to transmission case (M8) . . . . 23 Nm (17 ft-lb)

Tensioner spring to
speedometer sensor (M6) . . . . 10 Nm (7.5 ft-lb)

TRANSMISSION COMPONENTS

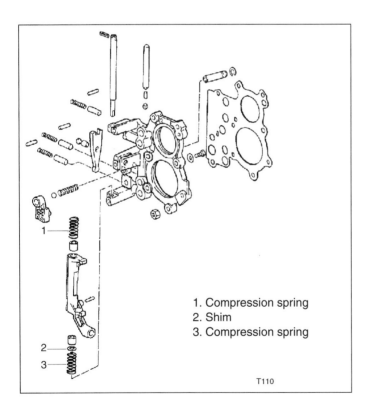

1. Compression spring
2. Shim
3. Compression spring

T110

Shift linkage

Note correct locations of compression springs.

Compression spring relaxed lengths
Spring **1**
 1989 - 1/1991 . . . . 33.9 ± 0.5 mm (1.13 ± 0.02 in)
 2/1991 on . . . . .63.0 ± 0.5 mm (2.48 ± 0.02 in)
Spring **3**. . . . . .55.2 ± 0.5 mm (2.17 ± 0.02 in)

Selector sleeve assembly

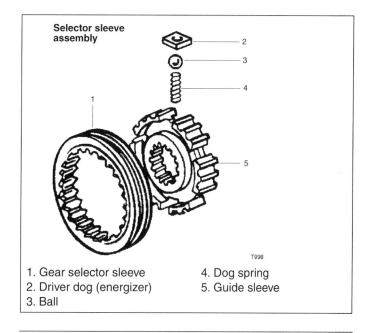

Selector sleeve assembly

T998

1. Gear selector sleeve
2. Driver dog (energizer)
3. Ball
4. Dog spring
5. Guide sleeve

Dog springs
Length
 1st/2nd gear spring . . . . . 10.7± 0.2 mm (0.42 ± 0.008 in)
 3rd/4th gear spring . . . . .11.8 + 0.3 mm (0.47 + 0.008 in)
Thickness
1st/2nd gear spring . . . . .0.9 mm (0.035 in)
3rd/4th gear spring . . . . .0.8 mm (0.03 in)

Selector sleeve spacing

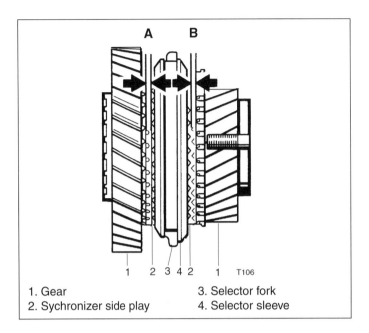

1. Gear
2. Sychronizer side play
3. Selector fork
4. Selector sleeve

Service note –

- When adjusting selector sleeve, be sure spacing for **A** and **B** are same.

Synchronizer wear

Inspect synchronizer rings for wear.

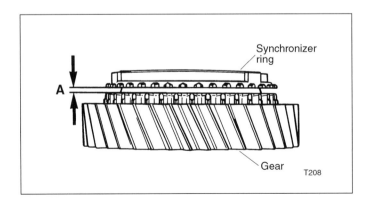

Service note –

- Press ring into gear wheel cone and measure gap **A**.

Synchronizer specifications

New synchronizer
  Gap **A** for 1st/2nd gears . . . . .min. 1.1 mm (0.04 in)
  Gap **A** for 3rd/4th gears. . . . . .min. 0.9 mm (0.035 in)
Wear limit
Gap **A** . . . . 0.6 - 0.7 mm (0.024 - 0.028 in)

Pinion bearing

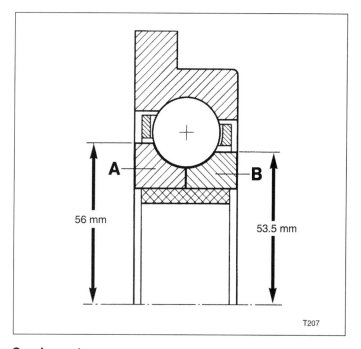

T207

Service note –

- Large inner pinion bearing race (**A**) must face pinion gear end of output shaft.
- Small inner pinion bearing race (**B**) must face 4th gear.
- Heat all bearings and bearing inner races to 120° C (248° F) before pressing on shaft.

TORQUE TRANSFER ASSEMBLY

Assembly at front of transmission transfers torque to center driveshaft and front final drive. Special Porsche service tools are required for transmission and torque transfer housing disassembly and reassembly.

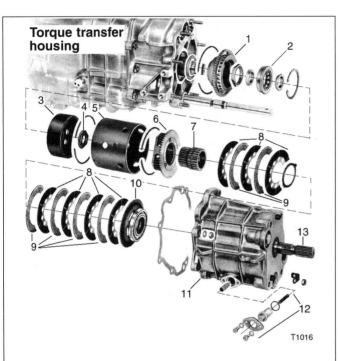

Torque transfer housing

T1016

1. Bearing carrier
2. Ball bearing
3. Clutch carrier
4. Output shaft collar nut
5. Clutch sleeve
6. Planetary wheel carrier
7. Sun wheel
8. Inner clutch discs
9. Outer clutch discs
10. Pressure plate
11. Transfer housing
12. Locking pin assembly
13. Output shaft

Tightening torque
Clutch carrier to output shaft
(M40 collar nut) .... 240 Nm (177 ft-lb)

Torque transfer clutch pack

Transfer housing clutch friction discs have been switched from Gylon® to Valeo®. Do not combine two types. Check with authorized Porsche dealer for latest parts information.

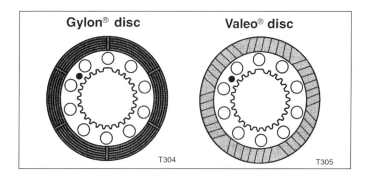

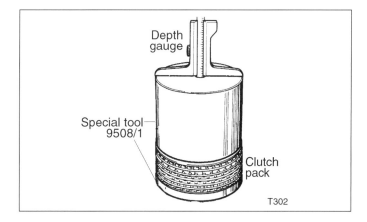

Service note –

• Use special tool 9508/1 to measure and set Valeo® friction pack height.
• If wear limit is reached, replace all inner (friction) discs.

Friction pack height

New Valeo® discs . . . . 26.0 - 0.2 mm (1.02 - 0.008 in)
Wear limit with used friction discs . . . . . .25.1 mm (0.99 in)

Pressure plate setting

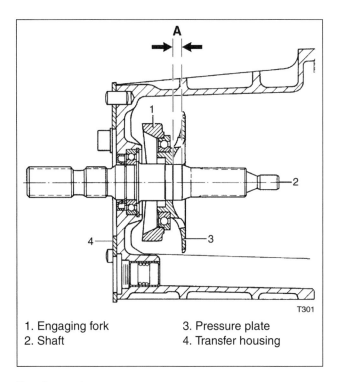

T301

1. Engaging fork   3. Pressure plate
2. Shaft   4. Transfer housing

Service note –

• Install clutch pack pressure plate in correct position. Recesses on pressure plate bearing must latch into driving journals of engaging fork.

Pressure plate placement

Dimension **A** . . . . .approx. 8 mm (0.315 in)

Counter-bearing adjustment

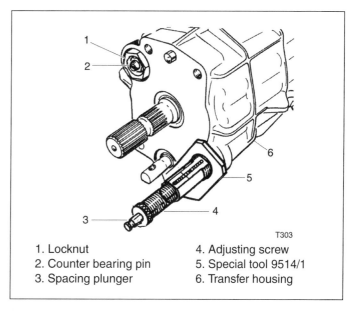

T303

1. Locknut
2. Counter bearing pin
3. Spacing plunger

4. Adjusting screw
5. Special tool 9514/1
6. Transfer housing

Service note –

• Use Porsche special tool 9514/1 to adjust counter-bearing for front-to-rear lock.
• Set adjusting screw to 29.5 mm (1.16 in).
• Set bearing pin to zero end play.
• Lock bearing pin with hex nut.

Tightening torque
Bearing pin locknut
(use Loctite® 222) . . . . 40 Nm (30 ft-lb)

37 Tiptronic Transmission
A50/01, A50/03

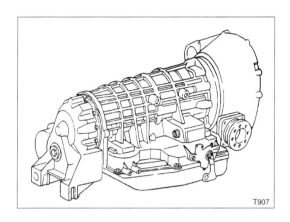

T907

37

GENERAL

A50 Tiptronic transmission is an option in Carrera 2 (rear wheel drive) cars. Tiptronic is a microprocessor controlled fully automatic 4-speed planetary transmission.

Transmission code example:
• **A5001 1 L 00941**

Explanation of digits and letters:
• **A5001**: Transmission type A50/01
• **1**: Variant: Normal differential
• **L**: Model year 1990 (not used as of 1992)
• 941st standard transmission installed

Transmission type	Variants	Model year	Serial number
A50/01	1 Normal differential	**L** 1990 **M** 1991 (no letter used from model year 1992)	**00941**

Transmission applications

Year	Type
1990 - 1991	A50/01
1992 - 1994	A50/03

Technical data

	A50/01, A50/03
Gear: 1st 2nd 3rd 4th Reverse Final drive	2.479 1.479 1.000 0.728 2.086 3.667
Final drive gear	Hypoid bevel gear with 15 mm offset
Stall speed	2300 ± 200

MAINTENANCE

Automatic transmission fluid (ATF) level

In 1994 ATF capacity was increased by 0.5 liters (0.53 qts) over previous models.

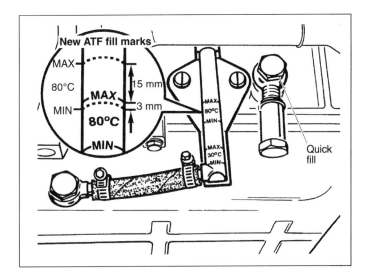

Reset MAX - MIN marks as follows:

- 1994 maximum: 15 mm (0.6 in) **above** 80°C (176°F) MAX mark
- 1994 minimum: 3 mm (0.12 in) **below** 80°C (176°F) MAX mark.

Service note –

- ATF level checking conditions:
  - Transmission splash shield removed, if applicable
  - Vehicle level
  - Engine idling
  - Parking brake applied
  - Selector lever in PARK position
  - ATF fluid temperature at 80°C (176°F). Determine using system tester 9288.

ATF and ATF strainer

Change ATF and clean ATF strainer every 40,000 km (24,000 miles).

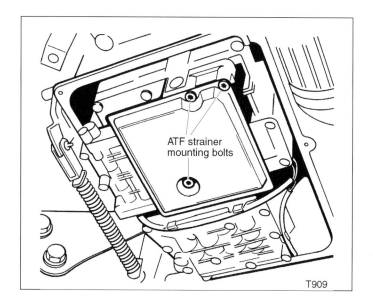

ATF strainer mounting bolts

T909

Transmission capacities

Automatic transmission fluid (ATF)
Complete refill . . . . .9.0 liters (9.5 qt)
ATF change . . . . .3.0 liters (3.2 qt)
Final drive . . . . .0.9 liters (0.95 qt)

Transmission oil specifications

Automatic transmission fluid (ATF) . . . . .Dexron II D
Final drive oil
Mineral based oil . . . . 75 W 90, API classification GL5
Synthetic oil . . . . MIL-L 2105 B

Tightening torques

ATF pan to transmission (M6) . . . . 10 Nm (7 ft-lb)
ATF strainer to valve body . . . . 8 Nm (6 ft-lb)
Drain plug to transmission pan (M14) . . . . 40 Nm (30 ft-lb)
Final drive oil drain or filler plug (M22) . . . 30 Nm (22 ft-lb)

ATF cooler

ATF cooler is ganged with engine oil cooler ahead of right front wheel, behind headlight housing.

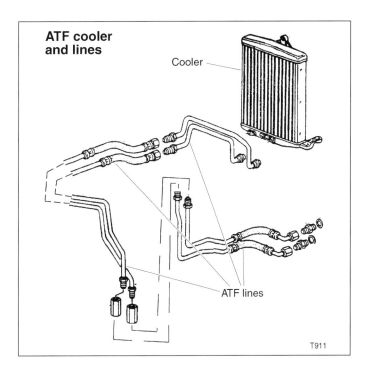

ATF cooler and lines

Cooler

ATF lines

T911

Tightening torques
ATF line connections . . . . 30 Nm (22 ft-lb)
ATF cooler to
  engine oil cooler . . . . 10 Nm (7 ft-lb)
Bracket to wheel housing . . . . 23 Nm (17 ft-lb)
Diagonal brace to bracket . . . . 10 Nm (7 ft-lb)
Retaining bracket to ATF cooler . . . . 6 Nm (4.4 ft-lb)
Retaining bracket to headlight housing . . . 23 Nm (17 ft-lb)
Retaining plate to retaining bracket . . . . . . 3 Nm (2.2 ft-lb)

TIPTRONIC TRANSMISSION ASSEMBLY

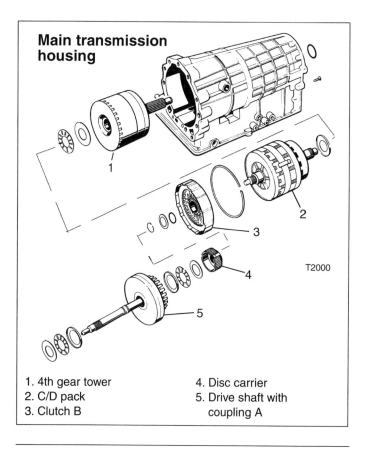

Main transmission housing

T2000

1. 4th gear tower
2. C/D pack
3. Clutch B
4. Disc carrier
5. Drive shaft with coupling A

Tightening torques

ATF indicator tube to transmission (M5) .... 5 Nm (4 ft-lb)
ATF drain plug to
  transmission pan (M14)............... 40 Nm (30 ft-lb)
ATF line plugs (M14) .... 25 Nm (18 ft-lb)
ATF pan to transmission (M6) .... 10 Nm (7 ft-lb)
ATF pump to transmission housing (M6)... 10 Nm (7 ft-lb)
ATF screen to valve body (M6) .... 8 Nm (6 ft-lb)
Banjo bolts to
  transmission housing (M14) .... 40 Nm (30 ft-lb)
Bearing cover to bearing assembly (M6) .. 10 Nm (7 ft-lb)
Differential to transmission (M10) .... 46 Nm (34 ft-lb)
Drive pinion bearing assembly to
front transmission cover (M8) .... 23 Nm (17 ft-lb)

Tightening torques (continued)

Drive pinion bearing assembly to
  housing (M10) . . . . 50 Nm (37 ft-lb)
Final drive oil filler or drain plug (M22) . . . 50 Nm (37 ft-lb)
Intermediate plate to transmission (M8) . . 23 Nm (17 ft-lb)
Joint flange to differential (M10) . . . . 46 Nm (34 ft-lb)
Joint flange to transmission (M8) . . . . . . 23 Nm (17 ft-lb)
Lock nut to helical gear (M40) . . . . 250 Nm (184 ft-lb)
Locking nut to bearing assembly (M36). 250 Nm (184 ft-lb)
Multifunction switch (M6). . . . . 10 Nm (89 in-lb)
Operating lever to selector shaft (M8) . . . . 15 Nm (11 ft-lb)
Parking lock guide to housing (M6) . . . . . . 10 Nm (89 in-lb)
Pressure regulator solenoid mount to
  control unit (M6) . . . . 5 Nm (44 in-lb)
Quick fill connector plug (M14) . . . . 30 Nm (22 ft-lb)
Rear transmission housing plug (M22) . . . 50 Nm (37 ft-lb)
Ring gear to
  differential (M10) (use Loctite®) . . . . 55 Nm (41 ft-lb)
Selector rod cable clevis (M5) . . . . 6 Nm (53 in-lb)
Solenoid valve to control unit (M5) . . . . 5 Nm (44 in-lb)
Switch plate to selector lever housing (M4). 2 Nm (18 in-lb)
Transmission cover to
  intermediate plate (M10) . . . . 46 Nm (34 ft-lb)
Transmission side cover to housing (M8) . 23 Nm (17 ft-lb)
Valve body to transmission housing (M6) . . 8 Nm (71 in-lb)

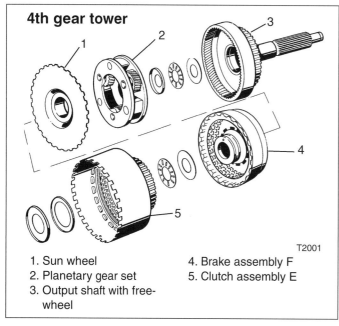

4th gear tower

T2001

1. Sun wheel
2. Planetary gear set
3. Output shaft with freewheel
4. Brake assembly F
5. Clutch assembly E

Output shaft and freewheel

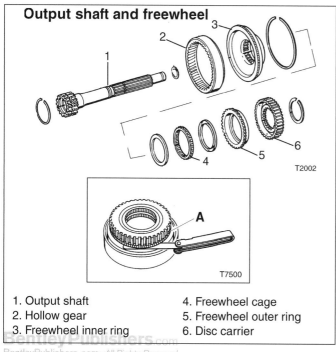

Output shaft and freewheel

T2002

T7500

1. Output shaft
2. Hollow gear
3. Freewheel inner ring
4. Freewheel cage
5. Freewheel outer ring
6. Disc carrier

Freewheel ring gap
Minimum gap
between inner and outer ring (**A**) . . . . . 0.1 mm (0.004 in)

CD brake pack assembly

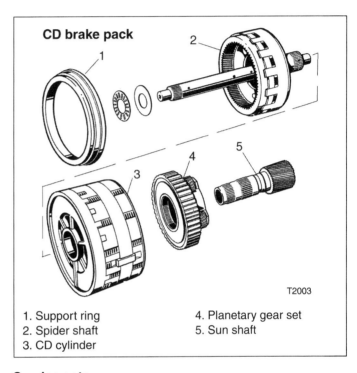

CD brake pack

T2003

1. Support ring
2. Spider shaft
3. CD cylinder
4. Planetary gear set
5. Sun shaft

Service note –
• Use special Porsche service tool 9314 to disassemble/re-assemble CD brake pack.

C, C' and D brake assemblies

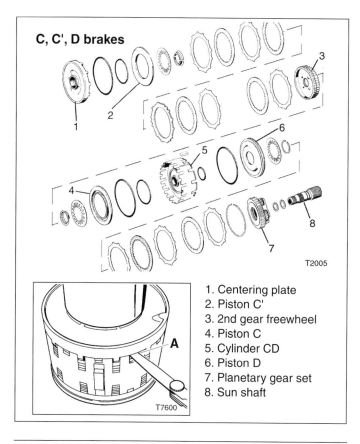

C, C', D brakes

T2005

T7600

1. Centering plate
2. Piston C'
3. 2nd gear freewheel
4. Piston C
5. Cylinder CD
6. Piston D
7. Planetary gear set
8. Sun shaft

Air gap specifications (A)

Brake pack **C**	0.63 - 2.40 mm (0.025 - 0.094 in)
Brake pack **C'**	0.55 - 1.97 mm (0.022 - 0.077 in)
Brake pack **D**	1.34 - 2.39 mm (0.053 - 0.094 in)

Spider shaft assembly

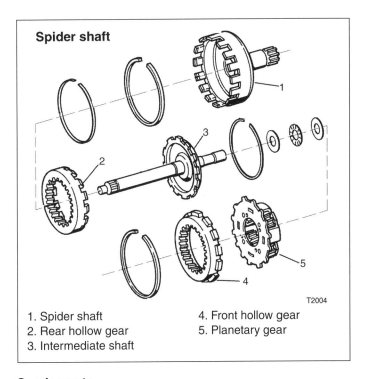

Spider shaft

1. Spider shaft
2. Rear hollow gear
3. Intermediate shaft
4. Front hollow gear
5. Planetary gear

T2004

Service note –

• Intermediate shaft must rotate freely after assembly.

Valve body

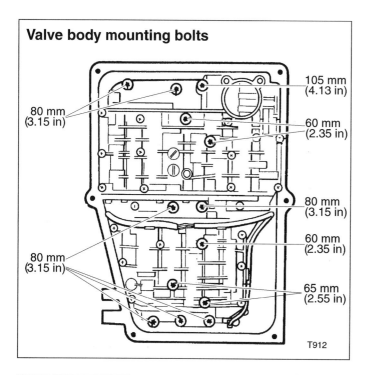

Valve body mounting bolts

105 mm (4.13 in)

80 mm (3.15 in)

60 mm (2.35 in)

80 mm (3.15 in)

60 mm (2.35 in)

80 mm (3.15 in)

65 mm (2.55 in)

T912

Tightening torques

Valve body to transmission (M6) . . . . 8 Nm (6 ft-lb)
ATF strainer to valve body . . . . 8 Nm (6 ft-lb)
ATF pan to transmission (M6) . . . . 10 Nm (7 ft-lb)
ATF pan drain plug (M14) . . . . 40 Nm (29 ft-lb)

ELECTRONIC CONTROLS

Tiptronic control unit

Self-diagnostic Tiptronic control unit is located under driver's seat, next to engine control module (ECM).

Shift strategy

Tiptronic control unit processes signals to/from components listed in accompanying illustration.

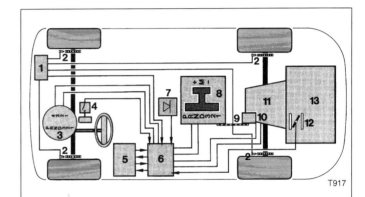

T917

1. ABS control unit
2. Wheel speed sensors
3. Speedometer
4. Kickdown switch
5. ECM
6. Tiptronic control unit
7. Transverse acceleration sensor
8. Selector lever
9. Cable
10. Position switch
11. Automatic transmission
12. Throttle potentiometer
13. Engine

Tiptronic control unit pin assignments

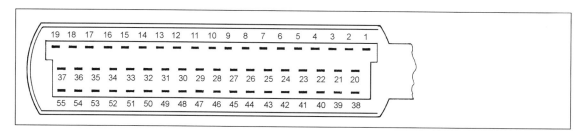

Pin	In/out	Connection	Function/comments
1	input	DME relay terminal 87 (fuse 27)	Battery voltage with ignition on, alarm off (terminal 15). Voltage interrupted when alarm on.
2	input	Transmission inductive pulse drive speed	Positive voltage signal
3	input	Battery	Battery voltage through fuse 35 (7.5 A)
4	input	Stop light switch	-
5	output	Solenoid valve I (SV1) switching point control	Ground signal to activate solenoid valve
6	output	Modulation pressure valve	Ground signal to activate solenoid valve
7	input	Ground location IV	Electronics ground
8	input	Throttle valve potentiometer	Variable voltage signal
9		Coding plug socket	Pin II
10	input	Selector lever switch	Indicates upshift
11	open	-	-
12	input	ABS control unit	Wheel speed signal (ESO) right front
13	output	Speedometer (pin 9)	Display manual operation
14	input	a. Transmission position switch b. Speedometer	a. Ground signal with shift level position IV b. Terminal VII on speedometer
15		ECM	-
16	output	Speedometer	Display 1st gear
17	open	-	-
18	open	-	-
19	output	Transmission solenoid valves	Battery voltage
20	output	Transmission inductive pulse sender	Ground shield for pulse sender harness
21		ECM (T 32), speed sender (T 22) with on-board computer	Load signal ITD
22	open	-	-
23	output	Automatic transmission light in dash	-

Pin	In/out	Connection	Function/comments
24	output	Solenoid valve 2	Ground signal to activate solenoid valve
25	output	2nd gear display	-
26	input	Ground location V	Ground for power consumers
27	input	Throttle valve potentiometer (T4)	Variable signal, depends on throttle plate position
28		Coding plug socket (T2)	-
29	input	Selector lever switch	Indicates downshift
30	input	Kick-down switch (T2)	Ground signal
31		Transmission diagnosis plug	-
32		ECM (T51)	Engine ignition adjustment
33	input	Speedometer position switch	Switch position Z pin 2
34	open	-	-
35	open	-	-
36	open	-	-
37	open	-	-
38	output	Transmission inductive pulse drive speed	Ground for pulse generator
39	input	Battery	Battery voltage through fuse 35 (7.5 A)
40		Lateral acceleration sensor (T2)	-
41	open	-	-
42	output	Converter lockup clutch	Ground signal to activate solenoid valve
43	output	Speedometer	Display 3rd gear
44		Throttle valve potentiometer (T5) Lateral acceleration sender (T1) Transmission temperature sender	Ground A/D converter
45	output	Throttle valve potentiometer	5 volts
46	input	Transmission temperature sensor	
47	open	-	-
48	input	Selector lever switch	Manual shift mode
49	output	Transmission oil cooler relay	Relay driver 2 speed oil cooler blower
50		Speedometer	Switch position
51		ECM (T55)	-
52	open	-	-
53	open	-	-
54	open	-	-
55	output	Speedometer	Display 4th gear

Solenoids and pressure regulator valve

Solenoid valves 1 (item no. 5) and 2 (item no. 6) are identical.

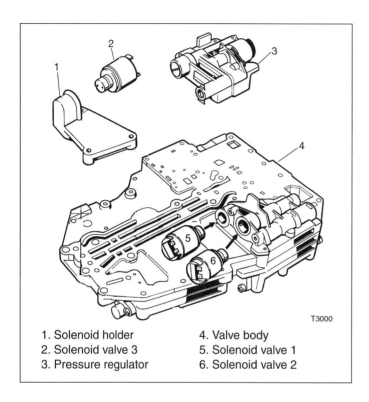

1. Solenoid holder	4. Valve body
2. Solenoid valve 3	5. Solenoid valve 1
3. Pressure regulator	6. Solenoid valve 2

Gear position switch

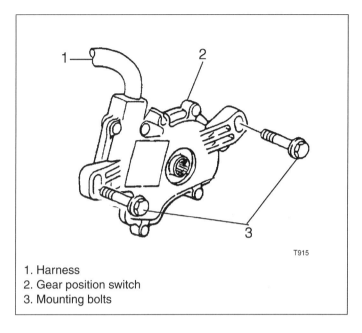

T915

1. Harness
2. Gear position switch
3. Mounting bolts

Service note –

• Use special Porsche service tool 9326 to center gear position switch during installation.

Tightening torques

Actuating lever to switch shaft . . . . 15 Nm (11 ft-lb)
Gear position switch to transmission . . . . 10 Nm (7 lb)

Transmission components in use

Selector lever position	Gear in use	Clutches in use			Brakes in use				Freewheels in use		
		A	B	E	C'	C	D	F	1st gear	2nd gear	3rd gear
D	1	X		X					x		X
D	2	X		X	X	X				X	X
D	3	X	X	X		X					X
D	4	X	X			X		X			
3	1	X		X					X		X
3	2	X		X	X	X				X	X
3	3	X	X	X		X					X
2	1	X		X					X		X
2	2	X		X	X	X				X	X
*1	1	X		X			X		(X)		X
R	R		X	X			X				

*Engine brake effective in overrun mode.

AUTOMATIC TRANSMISSION FAULT CODES

The Bosch 9268 tester or the Bosch 9288 tester can be used to access the Tiptronic fault memory. The Bosch 9268 is a simple flash (blink) code reader and the Bosch 9288 (also known as the "Hammer") is a more sophisticated tester.

Testers are connected to the 19-pin diagnostic plug in the right footwell. Adapter lead part number 9268/2 is required when using the Bosch 9268 tester. The Bosch 9288 tester plugs directly into the diagnostic plug.

Fault codes for Tiptronic system component failures are shown in the table below.

Service note –
• The diagnostic tool must be connected and disconnected with ignition off.

Bosch 9268 flashing code tester

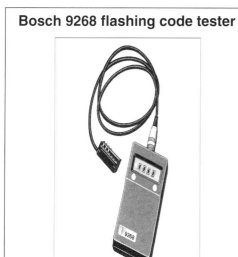

Bosch 9288 tester

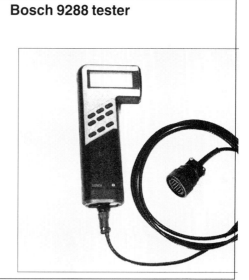

Tiptronic Transmission Fault Codes

Blink Codes (Bosch 9268)	Fault description (Bosch 9288 "Hammer")
11	Signal implausible
13	Voltage for drive links failed
14	Voltage for sensors failed
21	RPM signal from DME failed
22	Load signal from DME failed
23	Throttle potentiometer failed
24	Change of ignition timing
31	Solenoid valve 1 failed
32	Solenoid valve 2 failed
33	Solenoid valve torque converter clutch failed
34	Pressure regulator failed
35	Selector lever switch / transmission failed

Continued

Blink Codes (Bosch 9268)	Fault description (Bosch 9288 "Hammer")
36	Transmission speed sensor failed
37	Transmission temperature sensor failed
38	Selector lever switch / transmission partial failure
42, 43, 44	Transmission control unit failed
45 and 46	Downshift fault in rev limiter
51	Manual program switch failed
52	Tiptronic switch up and down failed
53	Kick down switch failed
54	Transverse acceleration sensor failed
55	Speed signal 1 from ABS control unit failed
56	Input to combination instrument failed
57	Transmission oil cooler blower relay failed
59	Switch R-position failed
60	Reverse light relay failed

39 Front Final Drive

Z64/00

T0015

GENERAL

Carrera 4 (all wheel drive) models are equipped with front differential and final drive. Special tools are required for differential disassembly and reassembly.

Technical data

	Z64/00
Gear ratio	3.444
Final drive gear	Hypoid bevel gear with 10 mm offset

Front final drive fluid

Recommended fluid. . . . . SAE 75 W 90 GL-5
Capacity. . . . . .1.2 liters (1.25 qts)

Tightening torques

Drive axle to front differential (M8) . . . . . . 42 Nm (31 ft-lb)
Drive flange to differential (M10) . . . . 44 Nm (32 ft-lb)
Lock nut to drive pinion (M33) . . . . 230 Nm (170 ft-lb)
Lock bolt to lock nut (M5) . . . . 6 Nm (4 ft-lb)
Oil filler or drain plug (M22) . . . . 30 Nm (22 ft-lb)
Ring gear to differential
  (M12 with tab washer) . . . . 150 Nm (111 ft-lb)
Ring gear to differential
  (M12 without tab washer) . . . . 200 Nm (147 ft-lb)
Side cover to differential housing (M8) . . . 23 Nm (17 ft-lb)

Front final drive components

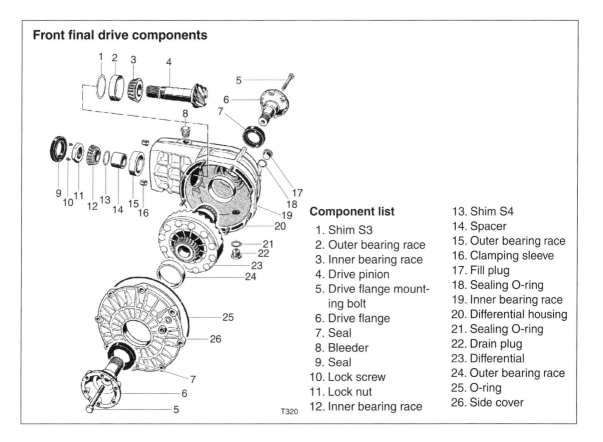

Front final drive components

Component list

1. Shim S3
2. Outer bearing race
3. Inner bearing race
4. Drive pinion
5. Drive flange mounting bolt
6. Drive flange
7. Seal
8. Bleeder
9. Seal
10. Lock screw
11. Lock nut
12. Inner bearing race
13. Shim S4
14. Spacer
15. Outer bearing race
16. Clamping sleeve
17. Fill plug
18. Sealing O-ring
19. Inner bearing race
20. Differential housing
21. Sealing O-ring
22. Drain plug
23. Differential
24. Outer bearing race
25. O-ring
26. Side cover

T320

Ring and pinion

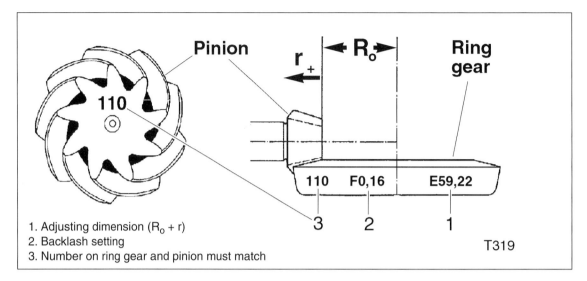

1. Adjusting dimension (R_o + r)
2. Backlash setting
3. Number on ring gear and pinion must match

T319

Drive pinion and ring gear are matched during production.

Service note –

- Shift drive pinion axially to achieve smooth, noise free operation.
- Keep ring gear within prescribed tooth-flank backlash tolerances.

Tightening torques

Ring gear to differential
(M12 with tab washer) . . . . 150 Nm (111 ft-lb)
Ring gear to differential
(M12 without tab washer) . . . . 200 Nm (147 ft-lb)

Central driveshaft tube

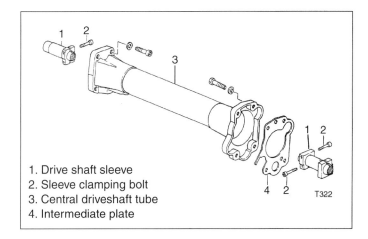

1. Drive shaft sleeve
2. Sleeve clamping bolt
3. Central driveshaft tube
4. Intermediate plate

T322

Tightening torques

Clamping sleeve to central
  driveshaft tube (M10) . . . . 75 Nm (55 ft-lb)
Drive shaft to transmission (M8) . . . . 42 Nm (31 ft-lb)
Driveshaft tube to transmission (M12). . . . 85 Nm (63 ft-lb)
Rubber seal ring to central
driveshaft tube (M6) . . . . 10 Nm (7 ft-lb)

40 Front Suspension

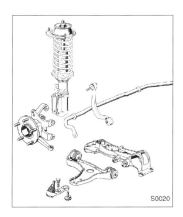

S0020

40

GENERAL

Front suspension design:
- Subframe crossmember and side members
- Lower control arms
- McPherson strut assemblies with coil springs

In Carrera 4 models, power is transferred to front wheels using two half-shaft axles with CV joints at each end.

Carrera 4 front wheel bearing carrier

Front wheel bearing carrier changed in 1990 models.

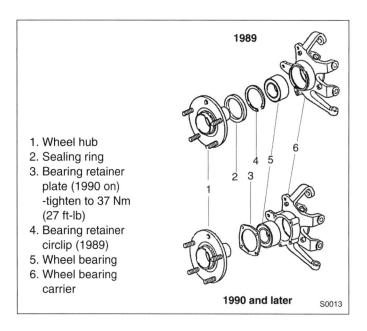

1989

1. Wheel hub
2. Sealing ring
3. Bearing retainer plate (1990 on) -tighten to 37 Nm (27 ft-lb)
4. Bearing retainer circlip (1989)
5. Wheel bearing
6. Wheel bearing carrier

1990 and later   S0013

Service note –
- It is possible to mix early and late design bearing carriers in same car without adverse effects.

Carrera 2 and Turbo front wheel bearing carrier

Front wheel bearing carrier for rear wheel drive models has been modified several times. Refer to illustration for most common configurations.

1. Wheel hub
2. Wheel stud
3. Spacer ring
4. Wheel bearing retainer bolts
   -tighten to 37 Nm
   (27 ft-lb)
5. Wheel bearing
6. Collar nut
   -always replace
   -coat threads and nut seating face with
   Optimoly®HT
   -tighten to 460 Nm
   (339 ft-lb)
7. Tensioner shim with ABS pulse wheel
8. Washer
9. Bolt
10. Stub axle with ABS pulse wheel
    (Carrera RS only)
11. Dust cap
12. Wheel bearing carrier

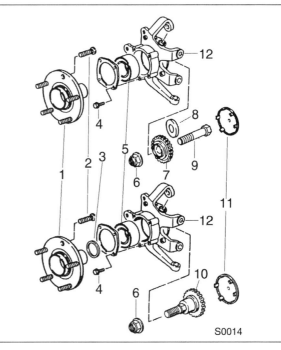

S0014

FRONT SUSPENSION

Front springs and stabilizer bar

Front spring identification
C4 . . . . orange marking
C2 / Turbo to 1991 . . . . blue marking
C2 / Turbo-look / RS America 1992 on . . . . green marking
Speedster (convertible) . . . . .green/white marking
Turbo 3.6 . . . . orange/green marking

Front stabilizer bar thickness
C4 1989 . . . . 20 mm
C2 / C4 1990 on . . . . 20 mm
C2 / C4 1990 on with M030 option package . . . . . . 22 mm
RS America / Turbo-look / Turbo 3.6 . . . . 21 mm

---

Service note –
• Replace stabilizer bar links and mounts if stabilizer bar is
  replaced with one of different design.

Carrera 4 front suspension

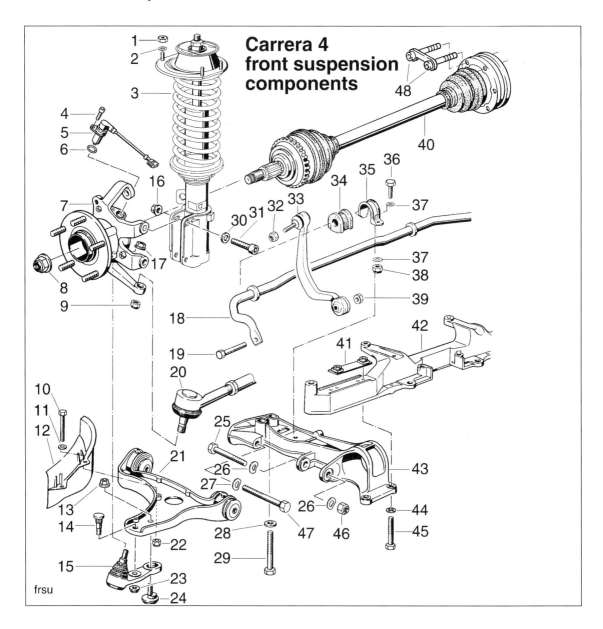

Carrera 4 front suspension components

Component List

1. Nut M8
   -coat with Optimoly®HT
   -tighten to 23 Nm (17 ft-lb)
2. Washer
3. Front strut assembly
4. Bolt M6
   -coat with Optimoly®HT
   -tighten to 10 Nm (7 ft-lb)
5. Wheel speed sensor
6. Sealing O-ring
   -always replace
7. Wheel bearing carrier
   -coat inner splines with Opti-moly®HT
8. Drive axle collar nut
   -always replace
   -coat threads and nut seating face with Optimoly®HT
   -tighten to 460 Nm (339 ft-lb)
9. Tie-rod end lock nut M12
   -coat with Optimoly®HT
   -tighten to 65 Nm (48 ft-lb)
10. Bolt M6
    -tighten to 10 Nm (7 ft-lb)
11. Washer
12. Brake air duct
13. Lock nut M10
    -tighten to 65 Nm (48 ft-lb)
14. Knurled bolt M10
    -coat with Optimoly®HT
15. Ball joint
16. Lock nut
17. Ball joint lock nut M12
    -always replace
    -coat with Optimoly®HT
    -tighten to 65 Nm (48 ft-lb)

18. Stabilizer bar
19. Bolt M10
    -coat with Optimoly®HT
20. Tie rod end
21. Control arm
22. Lock nut M6
    -tighten to 10 Nm (7 ft-lb)
23. Lock nut M10
    -tighten to 65 Nm (48 ft-lb)
24. Caster eccentric
    -coat seating face with Opti-moly®TA
25. Bolt M12
    -coat with Optimoly®HT
    -tighten to 85 Nm (63 ft-lb)
26. Spring washer
    -always replace
27. Washer
    -always replace
28. Washer
29. Bolt M12
    -coat with Optimoly®HT
    -tighten to 85 Nm (63 ft-lb)
30. Washer
    -always replace
31. Bolt M12
    -always replace
    -coat with Optimoly®HT
    -tighten to 135 Nm (101 ft-lb)
    -realign front end
32. Lock nut M10
    -always replace
    -tighten to 46 Nm (34 ft-lb)
33. Stabilizer bar link
34. Stabilizer bar bushing
    -coat with Texaco Omnis®32

35. Stabilizer bar bracket
36. Bolt M8
37. Washer
38. Nut M8
    -always replace
    -tighten to 23 Nm (17 ft-lb)
39. Lock nut M10
    -always replace
    -tighten to 46 Nm (34 ft-lb)
40. Half-shaft drive axle
    -coat splines with Opti-moly®HT
41. Threaded plate
42. Subframe crossmember
43. Suspension side member
44. Washer
45. M10 bolt
    -coat with Optimoly®HT
    -tighten to 46 Nm (34 ft-lb)
46. Lock nut M12
    -always replace
    -tighten to 85 Nm (63 ft-lb)
47. Bolt M12
    -always replace
    -coat with Optimoly®HT
    -tighten to 110 Nm (81 ft-lb)

Front strut assembly

Front strut assembly components

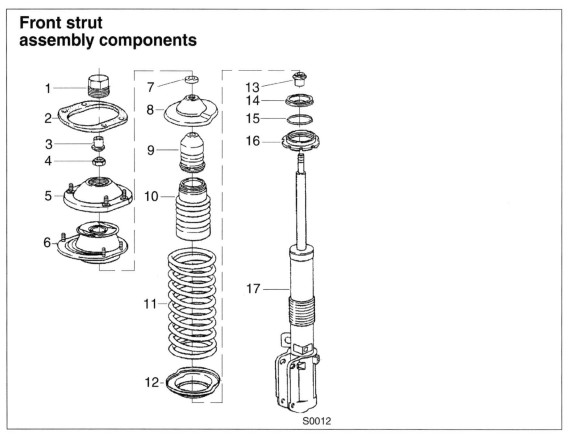

S0012

Component List

1. Strut mount cap (Carrera RS models)
2. Strut mount gasket
3. Strut rod lock nut M14 (Carrera RS models)
   -tighten to 80 Nm (59 ft-lb)
4. Strut rod lock nut M14 (1989 on)
   -tighten to 80 Nm (59 ft-lb)
5. Upper strut mount (Carrera RS models)
   -tighten to body 23 Nm (17 ft-lb)
6. Upper strut mount
   -tighten to body 23 Nm (17 ft-lb)
7. Spacer
8. Upper spring seat
9. Strut bump stop
10. Dust boot
11. Spring
12. Lower spring seat
13. Spacer (Carrera RS models)
14. Washer (Carrera RS models)
15. Gasket (Carrera RS models)
16. Lower spring seat adjusting nut
    -mark position and transfer to new strut
    -coat threads with Optimoly®TA
17. Strut
    -counterhold strut rod with 7 mm Allen key at top
    of rod to torque lock nut

Front upper strut mounting

Carrera 2, Carrera 4 and RS America models differ from Turbo and Turbo-look models in front upper strut mounting configuration. Install mounts as illustrated.

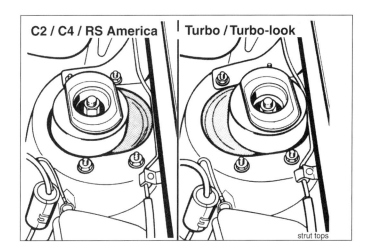

42 Rear Suspension

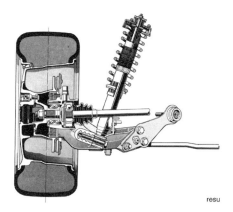

resu

42

GENERAL

Rear suspension overview

- Independent travel
- Trailing arms
- Oblique arms
- Stabilizer bar
- McPherson struts with helical springs

Rear stabilizer bar thickness

C4 1989.	18 mm
C2 1990.	21 mm
C2/C4 1991 on	20 mm
C2 with M249 option package	19 mm
Turbo/Turbo-look	22 mm
Turbo-look with M249 option package	21 mm

Rear suspension components

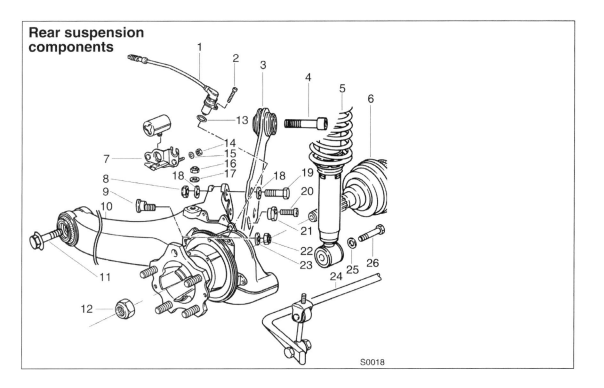

S0018

1. Wheel speed sensor
2. Bolt M6
   -coat with Optimoly®HT
   -tighten 10 Nm (7 ft-lb)
3. Oblique arm
   (rear axle spring brace)
4. Bolt M14
   -coat with Optimoly®HT
   -tighten 200 Nm (147 ft-lb)
5. Rear strut assembly
6. Half shaft drive axle
   -coat splines with Opti-
   moly®HT
7. Bracket with connector
8. Lock nut M14
9. Camber eccentric M14
   -coat seating face with
   Optimoly®TA
10. Trailing arm

11. Bolt M14
    -coat with Optimoly®HT
    -tighten 200 Nm (147 ft-lb)
12. Drive axle collar nut M22
    -always replace
    -coat threads and nut seating
    face with Optimoly®HT
    -tighten 460 Nm (339 ft-lb)
13. Sealing O-ring
    -always replace
14. Lock nut M6
15. Washer
16. Stab. bar lock nut M10
    -always replace
    -coat with Optimoly®HT
    -tighten 46 Nm (34 ft-lb)
17. Washer
18. Washer
19. Bolt M14

-tighten 200 Nm (147 ft-lb)
20. Bolt M12
    -coat with Optimoly®HT
    -tighten 58 Nm (43 ft-lb)
21. Toe eccentric
    -coat seating face with Opti-
    moly®TA
22. Lock nut M14
    -coat with Optimoly®HT
    -tighten 200 Nm (147 ft-lb)
23. Washer
24. Stabilizer bar
25. Washer
26. Bolt M14
    -coat with Optimoly®HT
    -tighten 200 Nm (147 ft-lb)

REAR STRUT ASSEMBLY

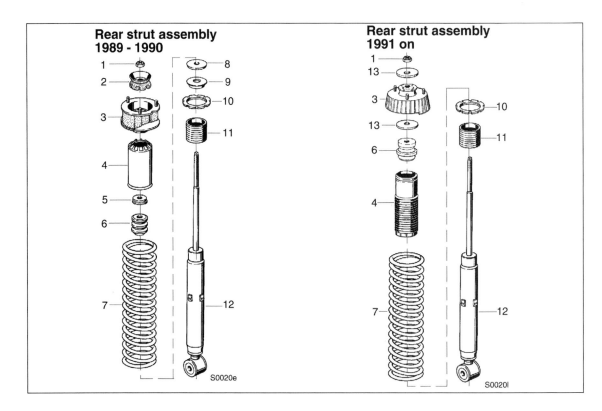

Rear strut assembly 1989 - 1990

Rear strut assembly 1991 on

1. Strut rod lock nut M12
   -always replace
   -coat thread with Optimoly®HT
   -tighten to 58 Nm (43 ft-lb)
2. Buffered washer
3. Upper strut mount
4. Dust boot
5. Support ring
6. Rubber bump stop
7. Coil spring

8. Thrust washer
9. Support cover
10. Lower spring seat adjusting nut
    -mark position and transfer to new strut (guide must point to spring)
    -coat threads with Optimoly®TA
11. Threaded bushing
    -coat threads with Optimoly®TA
12. Strut
13. Bowed washer

Upper strut mounting

Upper strut mounting to body redesigned for 1991 model year. Bowed washers used in upper strut from 1991 model year on.

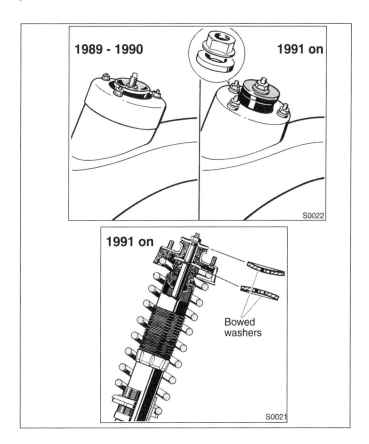

Service note –

• Replace springs in pairs only.

Upper strut mount fasteners (from 1991 models)
Collar nut . . . . .part no. 900.380.006.02
3.1 mm washer . . . . .part no. 999.025.125.02

Tightening torques
Strut mount to body
  1989 - 1990 models (M8) . . . . 20 Nm (15 ft-lb)
Strut mount to body
  1991 on (M8). 37 Nm (27 ft-lb)
Strut rod to strut mount (M12) . . . . 58 Nm (43 ft-lb)
Strut to lower control arm (M14) . . . . . . 200 Nm (147 ft-lb)

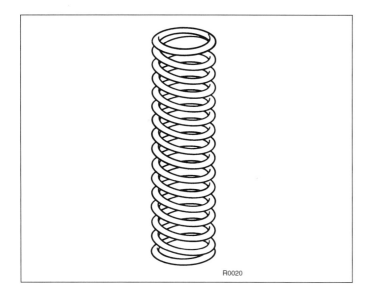

R0020

Rear spring identification

C4 / Turbo-look . . . . orange marking
C2 1990. . . . . blue marking
C2 91 on . . . . orange marking
Turbo 3.6 / C2 / C4
  with M030 option package. . . . . green marking
Turbo-look . . . . .violet marking

Note–
- M030 option package is only applicable to C2/C4 models built after October 31, 1990.
- M030 rear springs cannot be installed on C2/C4 cars built before November 1990.

REAR WHEEL BEARING HUB ASSEMBLY

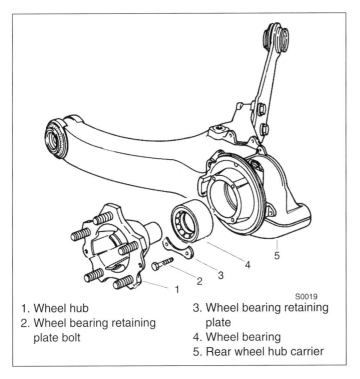

S0019

1. Wheel hub
2. Wheel bearing retaining plate bolt
3. Wheel bearing retaining plate
4. Wheel bearing
5. Rear wheel hub carrier

Service note –
- Use 31.3 mm diameter drift to press out wheel hub.
- Heat trailing arm to 120° - 150°C (248° - 302°F), press out wheel bearing and press in new.
- Use 40 mm diameter drift to support bearing inner race while pressing in wheel hub.
- Do not allow vehicle to rest on its wheel with drive axle removed.

Tightening torque
Wheel bearing retaining plate (M8) . . . . . . 20 Nm (15 ft-lb)

REAR DRIVE AXLES

Sizes of drive axle bolts (**arrows**) to transmission drive flange vary among models.

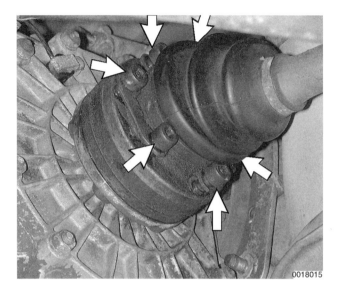

0018015

Service note –

• Clean inner hex surfaces of bolts prior to loosening/tightening.

Tightening torques

C/V joint to
   transmission drive flange (M8) . . . . 35 Nm (26 ft-lb)
C/V joint to
   transmission drive flange (M10) . . . . 44 Nm (33 ft-lb)
Drive axle to wheel hub (M22). . . . . 460 Nm (340 ft-lb)

44 Alignment, Wheels, Tires

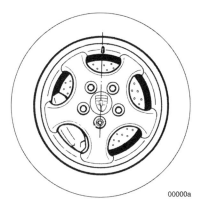

00000a

44

ALIGNMENT

Alignment specifications: C2 / C4 models

	Carrera 2 Carrera 4	Turbo-look	RS America Speedster
Ride height			
Front Max. left/right difference	175 ± 10 mm (6.89 ± 0.39 in) 10 mm (0.39 in)		
Rear (ground to outer trailing arm mount) 　　　(ground to cast boss on trailing arm) Max. left/right difference	280 ± 5 mm (11.02 ± 0.2 in) 268 ± 5 mm (10.55 ± 0.2 in) 10 mm (0.39 in)		
Front axle			
Toe, unpressed	+ 25' ± 5'		+ 15' ± 5'
Toe difference angle at 20° steering lock	- 40' ± 30'	- 1°20' ± 30'	- 40' ± 30'
Camber (with wheel in straight ahead position) Max. left/right difference	0° ± 10' 10'		- 15' ± 10' 10'
Caster Max. left/right difference	4°25' (+15', - 30') 15'		
Rear axle			
Toe-in per wheel Max. left/right difference	+ 10' ± 5' 10'	+ 15' ± 5' 10'	
Camber Max. left/right difference	40' ± 10' 20'	- 45' (max. -55', min. - 15') 20'	45' ± 10' 20'

Alignment specifications: Turbo models

	1991 - 1992 Turbo 3.3	1993 - 1994 Turbo 3.6
Ride height		
Front Max. left/right difference	175 ± 10 mm (6.89 ± 0.39 in) 10 mm (0.39 in)	
Rear Max. left/right difference	268 ± 5 mm (10.55 ± 0.2 in) 10 mm (0.39 in)	280 ± 5 mm (11.02 ± 0.2 in) 10 mm (0.39 in)
Front axle		
Toe, unpressed	+ 25' ± 5'	
Toe diff. angle at 20° steering lock	- 1°20' ± 30'	
Camber (wheel straight ahead) Max. left/right difference	0° ± 10' 10'	
Caster Max. left/right difference	4°25' (+15', - 30') 15'	
Rear axle		
Toe-in per wheel Max. left/right difference	+ 15' ± 5' 10'	
Camber Max. left/right difference	- 45' (max -55', min -15') 20'	

Note–
- Degrees symbol is °.
- Minute symbol is '.
- 60 minutes = 1 degree.

Wheel alignment checklist

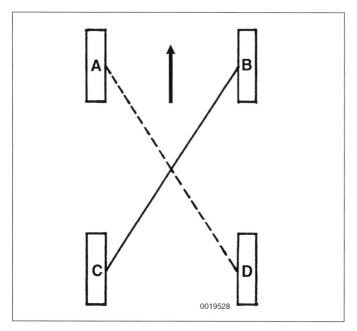

• Tire condition, pressures, tread depth acceptable
• Suspension parts wear acceptable
• Vehicle load and ride height correct

Vehicle height and wheel load

Adjust ride height by turning lower spring seat at suspension strut.

Measure wheel load using wheel load scales.

Changing ride height at one wheel will change load at all wheels. Wheel load changes are always transmitted diagonally to other side:

• Left front wheel (**A**) and right rear wheel (**D**) loads increase/decrease together.
• Right front wheel (**B**) and left rear wheel (**C**) loads increase/decrease together.
• Left/right wheel load tolerance < 20 kg (44 lbs)

Ride height

- Full fuel tank
- Spare tire and tools in vehicle
- Bounce suspension 2 - 3 times
- Car parked on level surface

Ride height

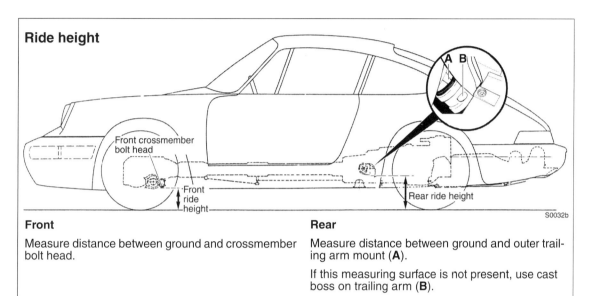

S0032b

Front

Measure distance between ground and crossmember bolt head.

Rear

Measure distance between ground and outer trailing arm mount (**A**).

If this measuring surface is not present, use cast boss on trailing arm (**B**).

Front camber

front camber

Service note –

- Bounce vehicle 2 - 3 times and allow car to reach normal ride height.
- Loosen upper and lower strut to wheel bearing carrier mounting allen bolts.
- Pivot upper bolt to adjust camber to specifications.
- Use Porsche special service tools 9265 and 9265/1 to pivot upper bolt and tighten in place.

Tightening torque
Strut to wheel bearing carrier
M12 Allen bolt . . . . 135 Nm (101 ft-lb)

Front caster

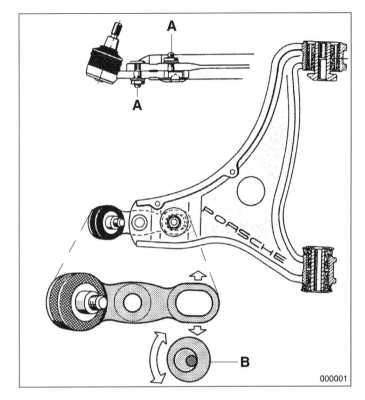

000001

Service note –

- Bounce vehicle 2 - 3 times and allow car to reach normal ride height.
- Loosen ball joint mounting bolts (**A**), then turn caster eccentric (**B**).

Tightening torques

Ball joint to control arm (M10) . . . . 65 Nm (48 ft-lb)

Front toe

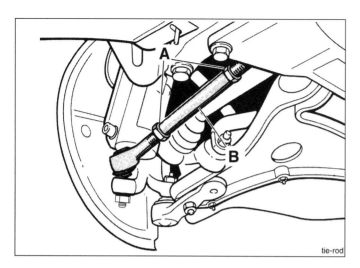

tie-rod

Service note –

- Bounce vehicle 2 - 3 times and allow car to reach normal ride height.
- Loosen tie-rod adjuster sleeve lock nuts (**A**).
- Turn adjuster sleeve (**B**) to change tie-rod length.
- Tighten lock nuts.
- Lengthen or shorten steering tie-rod on each side by same amount to keep steering wheel centered.

Tightening torque

Tie-rod adjuster sleeve lock nut. . . . . 45 Nm (33 ft-lb)

Rear camber and toe

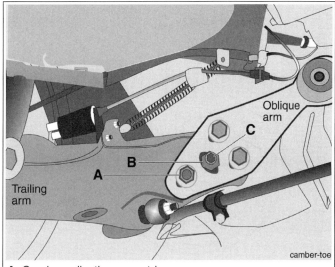

camber-toe

A. Camber adjusting eccentric

B. Toe adjusting eccentric

C. Toe adjusting eccentric mounting bolt

Service note –

- Bounce vehicle 2 - 3 times and allow car to reach normal ride height.
- Loosen camber eccentric (**A**), then adjust camber to specifications.
- Loosen toe eccentric mounting bolt (**C**), then adjust toe eccentric (**B**).

Tightening torques

Camber adjusting eccentric (M14) . . . . 200 Nm (147 ft-lb)

Toe adjusting eccentric (M12) . . . . 58 Nm (43 ft-lb)

WHEELS AND TIRES

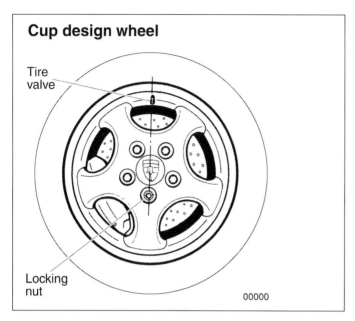

Cup design wheel

Tire valve

Locking nut

00000

Carrera 2/4 cars are equipped with a variety of wheels and tires.

Cup design wheels

Service note –

- Install 16" and 17" cup design wheels so that tire valve is opposite red-painted wheel stud. Then install locking wheel nut on painted stud.
- If unmarked, mark stud opposite valve before removing wheel.
- For stationary balancing (with stepped ring), run wheel so that valve points downwards. Tighten wheel in this position. After balancing, fit wheel to vehicle in same position (valve down, marked bolt and locking wheel nut up).

Note-

- Original 18" wheel (Turbo 3.6) has marked stud, tire valve and lockable wheel nut on same side.

Design 90, other wheels

Mount all wheels (other than cup design) with marked stud, tire valve and lockable wheel nut on same side.

When tightening, turn wheel so that valve points upwards (same position as on wheel balancer).

Tire pressures

Carrera 2 / Carrera 4 tire pressures
16 inch
   front (205/55 ZR 16) . . . . .2.5 bar (36 psi)
   rear (225/50 ZR 16). . . . . .3.0 bar (44 psi)
17 inch
front (205/50 ZR 17) . . . . .2.5 bar (36 psi)
rear (255/50 ZR 17). . . . . .2.5 bar (36 psi)
rear (275/35 ZR 17). . . . . .3.0 bar (44 psi)

Turbo and Turbo-look tire pressures
17 inch
   front (205/50 ZR 17) . . . . .2.5 bar (36 psi)
   rear (255/50 ZR 17). . . . . .2.5 bar (36 psi)
18 inch
front . . . . .2.5 bar (36 psi)
rear . . . . .3.0 bar (44 psi)

Snow tire pressures
16 or 17 inch
front . . . . .2.5 bar (36 psi)
rear . . . . .3.0 bar (44 psi)

46 Brake System

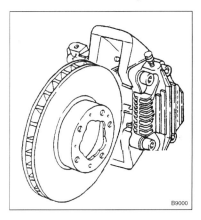

B9000

46

GENERAL

Major features of Porsche Carrera 2/4 and Turbo brake systems:

- 4-wheel disc brakes
- Dual hydraulic system
- Fixed caliper at each wheel
- Antilock braking system (ABS)
- C4/Turbo/Turbo-look models: Porsche Dynamic All-Wheel Control (PDAS) with hydraulic brake booster powered by ABS pump
- C2 models: Vacuum operated brake booster
- Cable operated parking brake shoes acting on brake drums integral to rear brake discs

Brake pad wear

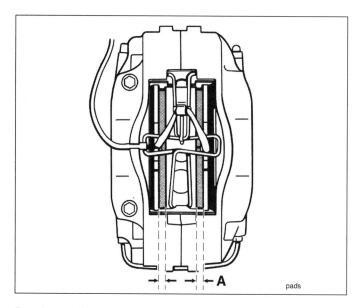

pads

Service note –

- Replace brake pads when:
  -Brake pad warning light on dashboard illuminates
  -Residual brake pad thickness (**A**) = 2 mm (0.08 in).

Brake fluid

Brake fluid reservoir

Service note –

- 1989 - 1992 models: Flush brake system and replace brake fluid every 2 years.
- 1993 and later models: Use DOT4 Plus brake fluid (Porsche part no. 000 043 202 04). Brake fluid flush and change interval is extended to every 3 years.
- Use Porsche system tester 9288 ("Bosch Hammer") to bleed and flush brake booster hydraulic fluid (Carrera 4 and Turbo models).
- Be sure to bleed clutch hydraulics while bleeding brakes.

Brake fluid specification
Fluid capacity
  Brake hydraulics
    C2 . . . . .0.34 liter (0.72 pt)
    C4/Turbo . . . . .0.75 liter (1.59 pt)
  Brake booster circuit (ABS). . . . . approx. 1.6 liter (1.7 qt)
Recommended fluid . . . . DOT4 Plus

Note–
- Porsche-recommended brake fluid has a higher boiling point than standard DOT4 fluid.

Tightening torques

ABS pressure pump to mount (M6) . . 10-13 Nm (7-10 ft-lb)
Bleeder valve
   to brake caliper (M10) . . . . 8 - 12 Nm (6 - 9 ft-lb)
Brake booster to bulkhead (M8) . . . . 23 Nm (17 ft-lb)
Brake caliper to wheel hub (M12) . . . . 85 Nm (63 ft-lb)
Brake disc backing plate
   to wheel hub (M6) . . . . 10 Nm (7 ft-lb)
Brake disc to wheel hub (M6) . . . . 5 Nm (4 ft-lb)
Brake line to brake system component
   (copper pipe) (M10). . . . . 12 - 14 Nm (9 - 10 ft-lb)
Brake line to brake system component
   (steel pipe) (M10) . . . . 14 - 16 Nm (10 - 12 ft-lb)
Brake pressure warning switch
   to pump (M25). 26 Nm (19 ft-lb)
Master cylinder to brake booster (M8) . . . 23 Nm (17 ft-lb)
Wheel speed sensor
   to wheel bearing hub (M6). . . . . .10 Nm (7.5 ft-lb)
Wheel to wheel hub (M14). . . . . 130 Nm (96 ft-lb)

BRAKE SYSTEM SPECIFICATIONS

Mechanical component specifications

Component	C2, C4, RS America, 911 Speedster	Turbo 3.3 Turbo-look (TL)	Turbo 3.6
Brake disc			
Diameter -front -rear	298 mm (11.732 in) 299 mm (11.772 in)	322 mm (12.677 in) 299 mm (11.772 in)	
Effective diameter -front -rear 2-piston caliper 4 piston caliper	248 mm (9.764 in) 252 mm (9.921 in) 246 mm (9.685 in)	268 mm (10.551 in) 249 mm (9.803 in)	259.6 mm (10.220 in) 249 mm (9.803 in)
Thickness (new) -front -rear	28 mm (1.102 in) 24 mm (0.945 in)	32 mm (1.260 in) 28 mm (1.102 in)	
Thickness (wear limit) -front -rear	26.0 mm (1.024 in) 22.0 mm (0.866 in)	30.0 mm (1.181 in) 26.0 mm (1.024 in)	
Brake disc			
Min. thickness after machining -front -rear	26.6 mm (1.047 in) 22.6 mm (0.890 in)	30.6 mm (1.205 in) 26.6 mm (1.047 in)	
Max. surface roughness after machining -max. thickness variance -max. lateral runout	0.006 mm (0.0002 in) 0.02 mm (0.0008 in) 0.1 mm (0.0039 in)		0.006 mm (0.0002 in) 0.02 mm (0.0008 in) 0.09 mm (0.0035 in)
Brake pads			
Surface area -front -rear	172 cm^2 (26.66 sq in) 2-piston: 112 cm^2 (17.36 sq in) 4-piston: 172 cm^2 (26.66 sq in)	250 cm^2 (38.75 sq in) 172 cm^2 (26.66 sq in) 422 cm^2 (65.41 sq in)	302 cm^2 (46.81 sq in) 172 cm^2 (26.66 sq in) 474 cm^2 (73.47 sq in)
Thickness -new -wear limit	12 mm (0.47 in) 4-piston rear caliper: 10 mm (0.4 in) 2 mm (0.08 in)	TL: 12 mm (0.47 in) Turbo front: 14.5 mm (0.57 in) Turbo rear: 12.5 mm (0.49 in) 2 mm (0.08 in)	12 mm (0.47 in) 2 mm (0.08 in)

Mechanical component specifications

Component	C2, C4, RS America, 911 Speedster	Turbo 3.3 Turbo-look (TL)	Turbo 3.6
Brake pedal pushrod clearance Brakes bled, engine stopped		Approx. 8 mm (0.3 in)	
Parking brake			
Drum diameter -new -wear limit		180 mm (7.09 in) 181 mm (7.13 in)	
Shoe width		25 mm (0.98 in)	
Liner thickness: -new -wear limit		4.5 mm (0.18 in) 2 mm (0.08 in)	

Hydraulic component specifications

Component	C2, RS America 911 Speedster	C4 Turbo-look (TL)	Turbo 3.3 Turbo 3.6
Brake booster Type Diameter Boosting factor	Vacuum operated 8 inches 3.0	Hydraulic (not applicable) 4.8	
Master cylinder Diameter Stroke	20.64 mm (0.813 in) 20/16 mm (0.787/0.630 in)	23.81 mm (0.937 in) 20/12 mm (0.787/0.472 in)	
Caliper piston diameter Front	2 x 40 mm (1.575 in) + 2 x 36 mm (1.417 in)	C4/C4TL: 2 x 40 mm (1.575 in) + 2 x 36 mm (1.417 in) C2TL: 2 x 44 mm (1.732 in) + 2 x 36 mm (1.417 in)	2 x 44 mm (1.732 in) + 2 x 36 mm (1.417 in)
Rear	2-piston rear caliper: 2 x 44 mm (1.732 in) 4-piston rear caliper: 2 x 30 mm (1.181 in) + 2 x 28 mm (1.102 in)	C4: 2 x 30 mm (1.181 in) + 2 x 28 mm (1.102 in) TL: 2 x 34 mm (1.339 in) + 2 x 30 mm (1.181 in)	2 x 34 mm (1.339 in) + 2 x 30 mm (1.181 in)
Brake pressure regulator Switch-over pressure	2-piston rear caliper: 45 bar (653 psi) 4-piston rear caliper: 55 bar (798 psi)	C4: 55 bar (798 psi) C2TL: 60 bar (870 psi) C4TL: 33 bar (479 psi)	60 bar (870 psi)
Reducing factor	0.46		

Note–
• C2TL (Carrera 2 Turbo-look) was badged "America Roadster" for the US market.

ANTILOCK BRAKE SYSTEM (ABS) AND TRACTION CONTROL SYSTEM

C4, Turbo, Turbo look, and RS versions were fitted with a hydraulic brake boost system. The C2, RS America and Speedsters used a vacuum boost system.

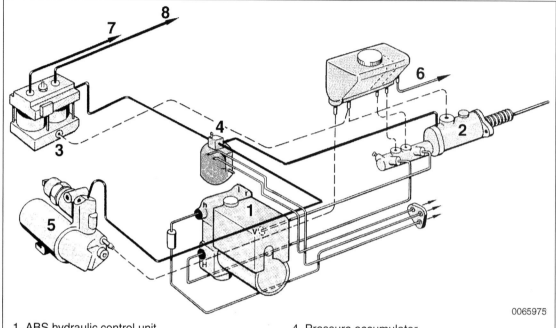

0065975

1. ABS hydraulic control unit
2. Brake master cylinder
   (master cylinder with hydraulic boost shown)
3. Solenoid valve body for axial and lateral lock
   solenoids (C4 models only)
4. Pressure accumulator
5. Hydraulic (boost) pump
6. Brake fluid reservoir
7. Hydraulic brake booster

ABS controls braking utilizing input from:
• Wheel speed sensors at each wheel hub

In Carrera 4 models with traction control (Porsche Dynamic All-wheel Control or PDAS), ABS control unit also receives input from:
• Lateral acceleration sensor
• Axial (front/rear) acceleration sensor

PDAS traction control activates axial and lateral lock sole-noids using hydraulic pump pressure.

Component locations

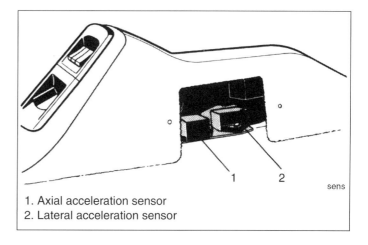

1. Axial acceleration sensor
2. Lateral acceleration sensor

Lateral and axial acceleration sensors
On sheet metal console on center tunnel. Remove access cover on right side of center console.

ABS hydraulic valve relay (A)
At ABS hydraulic control unit, behind battery in luggage compartment.

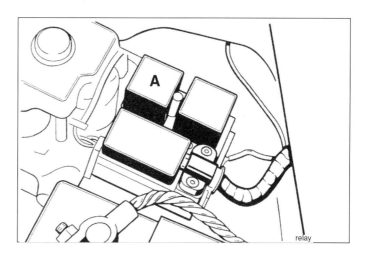

ABS pump relay (A)

Relay R51 in main fuse/relay panel in luggage compartment.

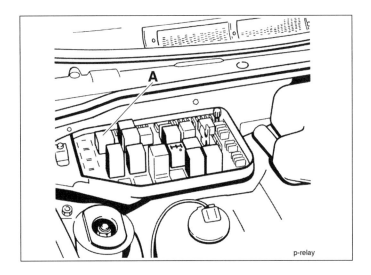

p-relay

Hydraulic pump

Left front luggage compartment.

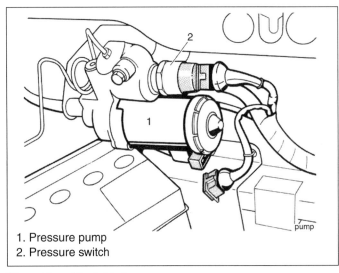

pump

1. Pressure pump
2. Pressure switch

ABS control unit ground (A)

Right side luggage compartment.

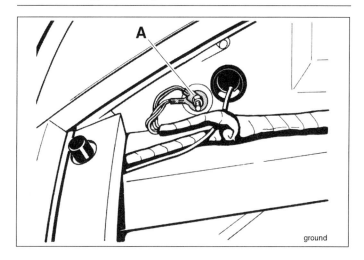

ABS control unit ground

ABS electronic control unit

Right front luggage compartment.

Wheel speed sensors

At each wheel bearing hub.

ABS control unit pin assignments

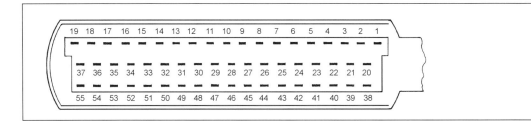

1. Voltage, terminal 15
2. Rear axle solenoid valve
3. Ground, right front solenoid
4. K-lead from diagnostic plug
5. Pump motor relay
6. Not used
7. Valve relay
8. Not used
9. Ground, acceleration sensors
10. Speed sensor output at right rear for rear spoiler aux. control unit.
11. Voltage, term. 30
12. Not used
13. Axial acceleration sensor
14. Not used
15. Power supply (+), acceleration sensors
16. Not used
17. Monitoring voltage, ABS solenoids
18. Longitudinal lock solenoid
19. ABS solenoid valve, left front
20. Power supply (+), valve and motor relays on hydraulic assembly

21. Transverse lock solenoid
22. ABS solenoid valve, right front
23. Monitoring voltage, lock solenoids
24. ABS warning light
25. Not used
26. Not used
27. D+
28. Full lock switch
29. Brake light switch
30. L-lead from diagnostic plug
31. Pump motor monitoring
32. Not used
33. Not used
34. Signal, transverse acceleration sensor
35. Lock warning light
36. Not used
37. Ground, left front, rear axle ABS solenoids
38. Not used
39. Not used
40. Pilot light for lock function at full-lock switch
41. Not used
42. Shielded ground, right rear

    wheel speed sensor
43. Signal, right rear wheel speed sensor
44. Shielded ground, left rear wheel speed sensor
45. Signal, left rear wheel speed sensor
46. Shielded ground, right front wheel speed sensor
47. Signal, right front wheel speed sensor
48. Shielded ground, left front wheel speed sensor
49. Not used
50. Not used
51. Signal, left front wheel speed sensor
52. Ground
53 - 55 Not used

48 Steering

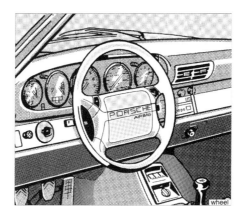

48

GENERAL

Carrera 2/4 and Turbo models are equipped with rack and pinion power-assisted steering.

1990 and later models are equipped with driver's airbag.

Caution–
- Observe airbag safety precautions when working at steering wheel or steering column:
  -Turn off ignition.
  -Disconnect battery.
  -Wait at least 20 minutes for airbag power supply to discharge.
- Do not disassemble or repair steering rack or fluid pump. Rebuilt exchange units are available from Porsche or aftermarket.

POWER STEERING

Power steering fluid

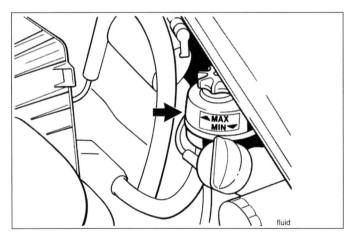

Service note –
- Use Dexron II D fluid in reservoir (**arrow**).
- Bleeding system:
  -Fill fluid reservoir to MAX mark then start engine briefly several times and switch off.
  -When fluid level in reservoir no longer drops, start engine and allow to idle. Turn steering wheel from lock to lock several times to release air bubbles. Do not pull on steering wheel more than necessary to turn wheels. Once fluid level stabilizes, top off.

Power steering belt

Power steering pump is mounted at right rear of engine, belt-driven by right camshaft. (Rear of engine is toward front of car.)

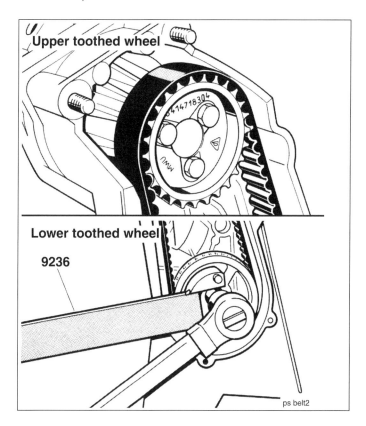

Upper toothed wheel

Lower toothed wheel

9236

ps belt2

Service note –

- To access power steering belt and check tension:
  - Remove final muffler and bracket.
  - Remove right engine top cover.
  - Remove belt guard.
- When replacing belt:
  - Fit upper toothed wheel with belt fitted.
  - Lettering on wheel must point to front of car.
  - Tighten lower toothed wheel to right camshaft while counterholding with special Porsche service tool 9236.
- Belt tension is not adjustable.

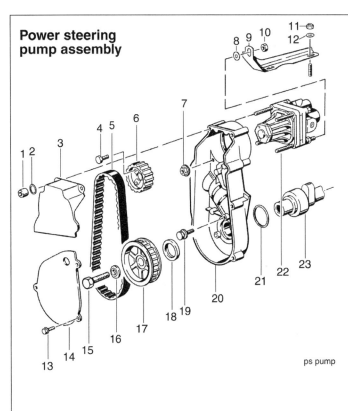

Power steering pump assembly

1. Allen nut M8
2. Spring washer
3. Cover
4. Bolt M6
5. Toothed belt
6. Toothed wheel
7. Collar nut
8. Washer M8
9. Mounting bracket
10. Nut M8
11. Lock nut M6
12. Washer
13. Bolt
14. Cover
15. Bolt M12
    -coat threads with Optimoly HT
    -tighten to 120 Nm (88 ft-lb)
    -use special Porsche service tool 9236 to counterhold while tightening
16. Washer
17. Toothed wheel
18. Sealing O-ring 30 x 42 x 7
19. Self-locking bolt M6
    -replace or use Loctite®270
20. Belt housing
21. Sealing O-ring 40 x 4
22. Power steering pump
23. End of right camshaft

ps pump

Tightening torques

Airbag to steering wheel	9.7 Nm (7 ft-lb)
Fluid lines to steering rack (M12)	20 Nm (15 ft-lb)
Pump toothed wheel to camshaft	120 Nm (88 ft-lb)
Pressure line to pump (M14)	30 Nm (22 ft-lb)
Pressure line to union (M14)	25 Nm (18 ft-lb)
Steering column to body (M6)	10 Nm (7.5 ft-lb)
Steering rack to crossmember (M8)	45 Nm (33 ft-lb)
Steering wheel to steering shaft (M16)	45 Nm (33 ft-lb)
Tie rod link fork to steering rack (M14)	70 Nm (52 ft-lb)
Tie rod to steering arm (M12)	65 Nm (48 ft-lb)
Tie rod to steering rack link fork (M14)	45 Nm (33 ft-lb)
Universal joint to steering shaft (M8)	23 Nm (17 ft-lb)

AIRBAG

Airbag removal

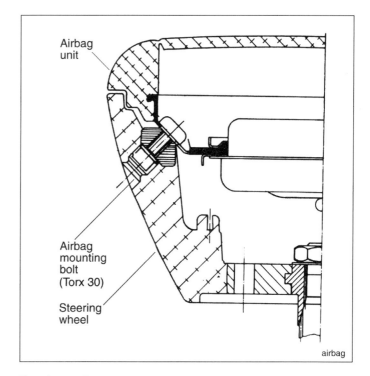

Airbag
unit

Airbag
mounting
bolt
(Torx 30)

Steering
wheel

airbag

Service note –

• Remove airbag mounting bolt installed diagonally on two
sides of steering wheel at front.

Caution–

• Observe airbag safety regulations when working at steer-
ing wheel or steering column:
-Turn off ignition.
-Disconnect battery.
-Wait 20 minutes for airbag power supply to discharge.

Airbag installation

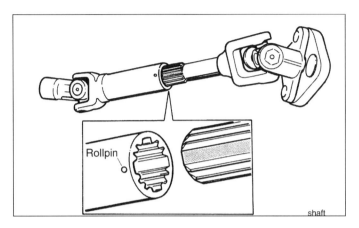

shaft

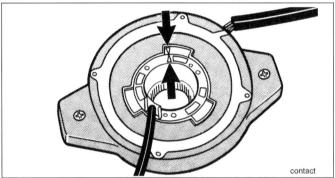

contact

Service note –

- If steering shaft has been slid apart, reassemble with roll-pin facing double spline.
- Point steering straight ahead before assembling universal joints.

If steering wheel is not marked before steering rack removal:

- Set airbag contact to center position with front wheels in straight ahead position.
- Airbag contact center is 4½ turns from full left or full right lock. Precise center position is indicated by **arrows**.

Tightening torque
Airbag to steering wheel . . . . .9.7 Nm (7 ft-lb)

TIE ROD ASSEMBLY

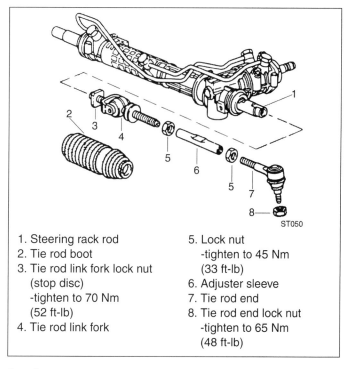

ST050

1. Steering rack rod
2. Tie rod boot
3. Tie rod link fork lock nut
   (stop disc)
   -tighten to 70 Nm
   (52 ft-lb)
4. Tie rod link fork

5. Lock nut
   -tighten to 45 Nm
   (33 ft-lb)
6. Adjuster sleeve
7. Tie rod end
8. Tie rod end lock nut
   -tighten to 65 Nm
   (48 ft-lb)

Service note –

- Counterhold steering rack rod to loosen or tighten link fork from rack or tie rod from link fork.
- Extend rack rod from rack only as far as necessary when loosening or tightening link fork or tie rod.
- Assemble so that tie rod end (**7**) and tie rod link fork (**4**) are screwed into adjusting sleeve approximately same number of turns.
- Coat fully extended steering rack rod with VW steering gear grease AOF 063 000 04.

Steering range

Adjust distance of fork lock nut/stop disc on steering rack to set lock-to-lock steering range.

Steering stop setting
Lock nut
to end of rack rod (**A**) . . . . 4 - 5 mm (0.16 - 0.20 in)

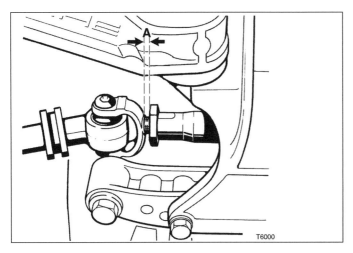

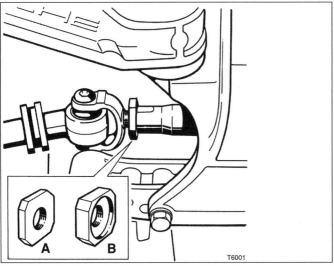

Steering travel limiter

Stop washer **A** . . . . 6 mm (0.24 in)
  -Standard on 1989 - 1991 models
Stop washer **B** . . . . 10 mm (0.4 in)
-Standard on 1992 and later models
-Install in pre-1992 models if fitting with 17 inch or larger wheels.

87 Air Conditioning

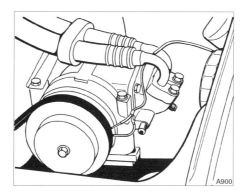

A900

87

GENERAL

Use special equipment to evacuate and recharge R12 and R134a A/C systems.

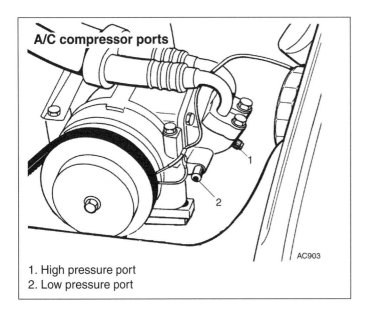

A/C compressor ports

1. High pressure port
2. Low pressure port

A/C system capacities

R12 refrigerant (1989 - 1992) . . . . 930 g (2.05 lb)
R134a refrigerant (1993 - 1994) . . . . 840 g (1.85 lb)
Compressor oil:
Densoil (1989 - 1992) . . . . 100 ± 20 cm³ (3.4 ± 0.7 oz)
ND 8 (1993 - 1994) . . . . 140 ± 20 cm³ (4.7 ± 0.7 oz)

Tightening torques

A/C compressor adjusting plate
   to mount . . . . 22 Nm (17 ft-lb)
A/C compressor clutch
   to compressor shaft. . . . . 16 Nm (12 ft-lb)
A/C compressor to adjusting plate. . . . . . . 28 Nm (21 ft-lb)
Refrigerant lines to expansion valve or evaporator
5/8" fitting . . . . 17 ± 3 Nm (13 ± 2 ft-lb)
3/4" fitting . . . . 24 ± 4 Nm (18 ± 3 ft-lb)
7/8" fitting . . . . 33 ± 4 Nm (24 ± 3 ft-lb)

A/C COMPONENTS

Component locations

A/C compressor relay . . . . . . left rear engine compartment
A/C-heating control unit. . . . . center of dashboard

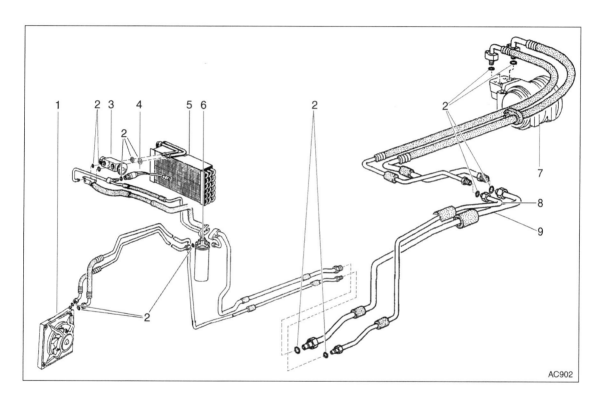

AC902

1. Condenser and fan
2. Sealing O-rings
   -always replace
3. Expansion valve
4. Pressure switch
5. Evaporator
6. Receiver-dryer

7. Compressor
8. High pressure line
9. Low pressure line
   -tighten refrigerant lines:
   5/8" 17 ± 3 Nm (13 ± 2 ft-lb)
   3/4" 24 ± 4 Nm (18 ± 3 ft-lb)
   7/8" 33 ± 4 Nm (24 ± 3 ft-lb)

Service note –

• On 1991 and earlier models, modify A/C control unit wiring harness (added jumper wire) prior to installing new control unit with part number index 01. See illustration below.

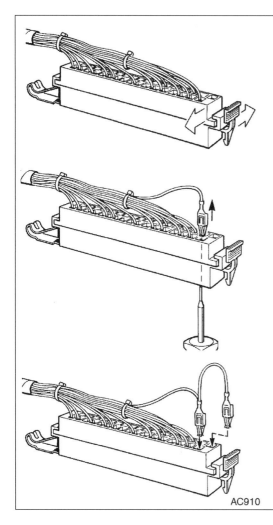

1. Pull off 35-pin harness connector (connector G) at A/C control unit.
2. Take G connector apart
3. Detach terminal G19.
4. Create Y-connection with 0.75 mm wire, length approx. 60 mm.
5. Reconnect to terminals G1 and G19

AC910

Compressor clutch

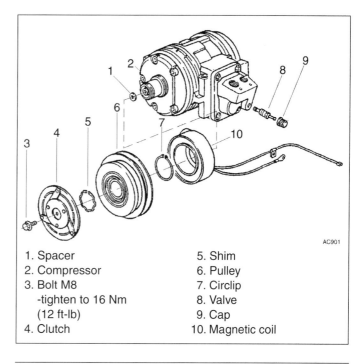

AC901

1. Spacer
2. Compressor
3. Bolt M8
   -tighten to 16 Nm
   (12 ft-lb)
4. Clutch

5. Shim
6. Pulley
7. Circlip
8. Valve
9. Cap
10. Magnetic coil

Clutch characteristics

Magnetic coil resistance . . . . 3.8 ± 0.2 Ω
Clutch drive plate
to pulley gap . . . . 0.4 - 0.7 mm (0.016 - 0.028 in)

A/C DIAGNOSIS

General requirements for testing A/C system:
- A/C drive belt tensioned correctly
- Magnetic clutch engaged
- A/C condenser clean
- Sunroof, doors, windows closed
- A/C running, cooling set to maximum
- Fresh air blower set to high

Service note –

- Run A/C approx. 10 minutes at engine speed of 2000 rpm. System tests can also be run with Porsche tester 9288 ("Bosch Hammer").
- Test cooling efficiency by inserting thermometer in center vent with A/C on. Center vent temperature specifications given below.

Center vent temperature

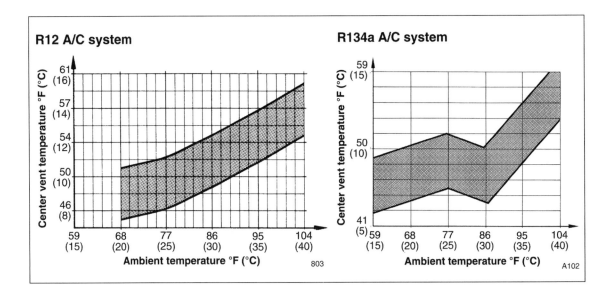

R12 A/C system pressure

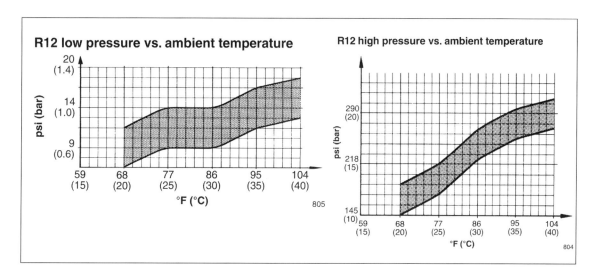

R12 low pressure vs. ambient temperature
R12 high pressure vs. ambient temperature

R134a A/C system pressure

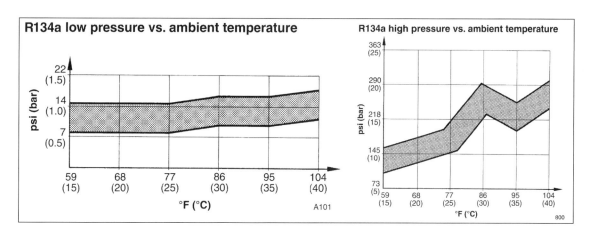

R134a low pressure vs. ambient temperature
R134a high pressure vs. ambient temperature

90 Electrical System

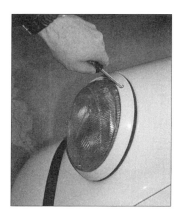

GENERAL

Fuse and relay locations

Fuses and relays are located in
• Main fuse/relay panel in right rear luggage compartment
• On steering column
• Under dashboard
• Fuse/relay panel left of engine
• Under front seats

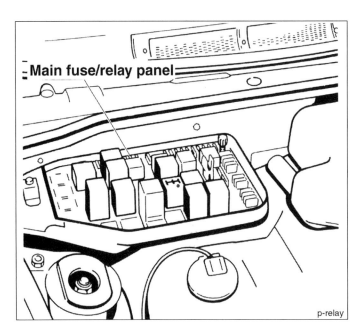

p-relay

Caution–
• Disconnect battery negative (-) cable and cover battery terminal with insulating material when working on electrical or engine management components.
• Connect and disconnect ignition system wires, multiple connectors, and ignition test equipment leads only while ignition is switched off.
• Use only a digital multimeter for electrical tests.
• Relay and fuse positions are subject to change and may vary from car to car. If questions arise, an authorized Porsche dealer is best source for accurate and up-to-date information.

Common bulbs

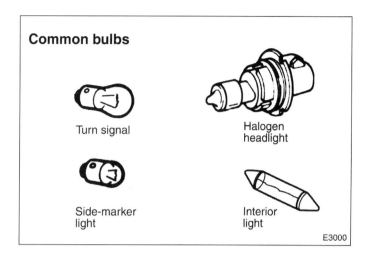

Turn signal

Halogen headlight

Side-marker light

Interior light

E3000

Bulb ratings

Ashtray light. . . . . 1.2 W
Back-up light . . . . .21 W
Engine compartment light . . . . .10 W
Foglight . . . . .55 W
Glove compartment light . . . . .10 W
Headlight H4 . . . . 60/55 W
Instrument bulbs . . . . 1.5 W, 0.9 W
Interior light . . . . .10 W
License plate lights
   C2/C4 . . . . .5 W
   Turbo . . . . 3.6 W
Luggage compartment light. .10 W
Running light, front . . . . .4 W
Side markers
   front. . . . . .5 W
   rear . . . . .4 W
Tail/stop light . . . . 21/5 W
Third brake light. . . . . .21 W
Turn signal. . . . . .21 W

GROUNDS, FUSES, RELAYS

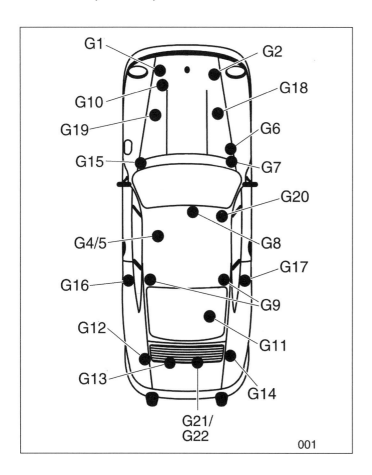

001

Ground locations

Ground	Location	Function
G1	Luggage compartment, left wheel housing	
G2	Luggage compartment, right wheel housing	
G3	Firewall	
G4	Under left seat	Power consumers

Ground	Location	Function
G5	Under left seat	Electronics
G6	Right rear luggage compartment	Main fuse/relay panel
G7	Right rear luggage compartment	Antenna amplifier
G8	Top center of windshield (convertible only)	Interior lights
G9	Above doors	Interior lights
G10	Left front luggage compartment	Battery
G11	Ground strap	Starter, transmission, engine, body
G12	Left rear engine compartment	
G13	Left side engine	
G14	Right rear engine compartment	
G15	Left windshield support	Instruments
G16	Combined lead, left rear	
G17	Combined lead, right rear	
G18	Combined lead, right front	
G19	Combined lead, left front	
G20	Under right seat	
G21/G22	At crankcase	Electronics

Main fuse/relay panel

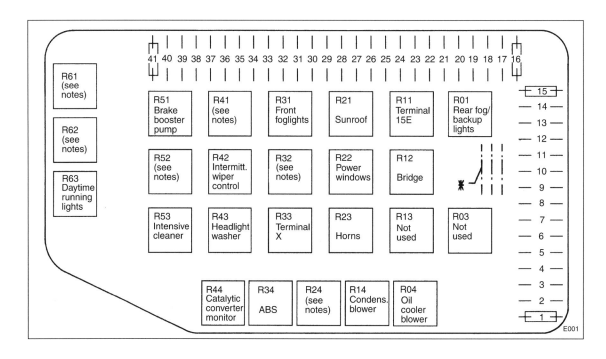

Fuse list

Fuse	Rating	Function
1.	25 A	Heater blower
2.	25 A	Oil cooler blower
3.	15 A	Horns
4.	30 A	Power windows
5.		not used
6.	30 A	Right power seat
7.	25 A	Cigar lighter
8.	30 A	Left power seat
9.	15 A	Emerg. flasher (USA)
10.		not used
11.	7.5 A	Interior lights, clock
12.	15 A	Diagnosis, central locking, rear window wiper
13.	25 A	Sunroof, electric convertible top
14.	15 A	Foglights, back-up lights
15.	40 A	Power brake booster pump
16.	15 A	Antilock system/limited slip differential
17.	7.5 A	Heater control
18.	7.5 A	Instruments, diagnostic plug
19.	15 A	Stop lights, cruise control
20.	7.5 A	High beam left
21.	7.5 A	High beam right

Fuse	Rating	Function
22.	7.5 A	Low beam left
23.	7.5 A	Low beam right
24.	25 A	Windshield wipers/washer,headlight washer
25.	25 A	Seat heater
26.	15 A	Turbo: front fuel pump C2/C4: not used
27.	15 A	Turbo: rear fuel pump C2/C4: not used
28.	15 A	Control unit, rear defogger, mirror adjustment, rear wiper
29.		not used
30.	7.5 A	Turn signals left rear, left side
31.	7.5 A	Turn signal left front
32.	7.5 A	Turn signal right front
33.	7.5 A	Turn signal right rear, right side
34.	15 A	C2/C4: fuel pump, oxygen sensor Turbo: not used
35.	7.5 A	C2/C4: DME Turbo: not used
36.	7.5 A	License plate lights

Fuse	Rating	Function
37.	15 A	C2/C4: Rear spoiler Turbo: not used
38.	15 A	Radio, amplifier
39.	25 A	Condenser blower (A/C)
40.	7.5 A	Left side marker light
41.	7.5 A	Right side marker light

Relay notes

42. R24
   1989 - 1990 C2/C4: not used
   1991 - 1994 C2/C4: ECM freq. converter
   Turbo: not used
43. R32
   1989 - 1990: Emerg. flasher
   1991 - 1994: not used
44. R41
   C2/C4: Main/fuel pump relay
   Turbo: not used
45. R52
   C2/C4: ECM freq. converter
   Turbo: Oxy. sensor system
46. R61
   C2/C4: Starting relay
   Turbo: Fuel pumps
47. R62
   Telephone fuses:
   Terminal 15 fuse: 5 A
   Terminal 30 fuse: 15A
48. R63
   Daylight running lights:
   Canada models only

Engine compartment fuse/relay panel

On Turbo models, auxiliary fuse/relay panel on left side of
engine compartment contains EZ69 ignition control unit.

Fuses in engine compartment fuse/relay panel
Heated rear window. . . . . 25 A
Rear heater blower (C2/C4 models) . . . . 30 A
Rear heater blowers (Turbo models) . . . . .two 25 A
A/C compressor. . . . . 7.5 A

Relays in engine compartment fuse/relay panel
Rear heater blower(s)
Heated rear window

ELECTRICAL COMPONENT LOCATIONS

Note–
- In "model" column, C2/C4 implies RS America models as well.

Component	Model	Location
15°C temperature switch	Turbo	On right timing chain housing cover
35°C temperature switch	Turbo	On crankcase vent cover
A/C blower switch	All	Left side of A/C-heater control panel
A/C clutch	All	Right side of engine, mounted on A/C compressor
A/C compressor relay	All	Engine compartment fuse/relay panel
A/C condenser blower	All	Left front wheel housing
A/C condenser blower relay (R14)	All	Main fuse/relay panel
A/C condenser blower resistor	All	Left front wheel well
A/C evaporator blower	All	Center of luggage compartment, under access panel
A/C pressure switch	All	Rear of luggage compartment at A/C line
A/C temperature switch	All	Right side of A/C-heater control panel
A/C-heating blower motor final stage	All	Luggage compartment, rear
A/C-heating blower motor, front, left/right	All	Luggage compartment, left/right
A/C-heating control unit	All	Under center dashboard
ABS control unit	All	Right front luggage compartment
ABS hydraulic control unit	All	Left front luggage compartment
ABS pressure switch	C2/C4	Front of luggage compartment
ABS relay (R34)	All	Main fuse/relay panel
Acceleration enrichment control unit	Turbo	Under left seat
Additional blower	C2/C4	Engine compartment, left
Air flow sensor		*see* Volume air flow sensor
Airbag control unit	All	Under center dashboard
Airbag, driver	All	In steering wheel
Airbag, passenger	All	In right side dashboard
Alarm horn	All	Right front wheel well
Alarm system control switches	All	Right and left door handles
Alarm system/central locking control unit	All	Under right seat
Alternator (generator)	All	Rear of engine behind cooling fan

Component	Model	Location
Altitude correction switch		*see* Pressure sensor
Antenna amplifier	All	Luggage compartment, right hood hinge area
Automatic heating control	All	Left side of A/C-heating control panel
Auxiliary air regulator	Turbo	Between cylinders 5 and 6 intake runners
Auxiliary fuse/relay panel	All	Engine compartment left side
Axial acceleration sensor	C4	Under center console
Back-up light relay	C2/C4	Luggage compartment left rear *see also* Rear foglight/back-up lights relay (R01)
Back-up light switch	All	Right side transmission
Battery	All	Left front luggage compartment
Battery switch	RS America	Front luggage compartment
Blower		*see* A/C condenser blower *see also* A/C evaporator blower *see also* A/C-heating blower motor, front, left/right *see also* Additional blower *see also* Heater blower, rear, left/right
Booster, radio	All	Under right seat
Brake booster pump	All	Luggage compartment front
Brake booster pump relay (R51)	All	Main fuse/relay panel
Brake fluid level switch	All	In brake master cylinder cap
Brake light switch	All	On pedal cluster under trim panel
Brake pad sensor	All	Inner brake pad, each wheel
Buzzer contact	All	In ignition switch lock
Central electrics		*see* Main fuse/relay panel
Central informer	All	On steering column
Central locking control unit		*see* Alarm system/central locking control unit
Charge air temperature sensor	Turbo	On engine
Clock	All	Dashboard, right side
Clutch switch for cruise control	All	On pedal cluster under trim panel
Codes plug, research octane number	Turbo	Left side engine compartment
Coil, ignition	All	Left side engine compartment
Cold start valve (injector)	Turbo	Left intake runners
Condenser blower relay (R14)	C2/C4	Main fuse/relay panel
Convertible top control microswitch	Convertible	Behind right rear trim panel (behind right door)

Component	Model	Location
Convertible top control unit	Convertible	Behind left side dashboard
Convertible top indicator light	Convertible	In clock
Convertible top lock microswitch, left/right	Convertible	In convertible top, center left/center right
Convertible top lock motor, left/right	Convertible	In top frame, center left/center right
Convertible top microswitch TDC	Convertible	Behind right rear trim panel (behind right door)
Convertible top motor left/right	Convertible	Behind rear seat backrest, left/right
Convertible top switch	Convertible	Above ignition switch
Crash sensor, left/right	All	Left/right strut tower in luggage compartment
Cruise control actuator	C2/C4	On engine, left side
Cruise control pedal switches	C2/C4	At pedal cluster
Cruise control switch	C2/C4	Right side steering column
Cruise control unit	C2/C4	Under right seat
Cruise control unit	C2/C4	Under right front seat
Cylinder head temperature sensor	All	Cylinder head 3
Daytime running light relay (R63)	Canada	Main fuse/relay panel
Defogger	All	*see* Rear window defogger
Defroster blower	All	*see* Windshield defroster blower
Diagnostic connector plug	All	In right footwell
Distributor(s)	All	Left side of crankcase behind crankshaft pulley
DME control unit	C2/C4	Under left seat
DME/fuel pump relay		*see* Main/fuel pump relay,
Door contact switch, left/right	All	Door hinge post, left/right
Door lock microswitch, left/right	All	On door latch, left/right
Door lock motor, left/right	All	Bottom rear of door
Emergency flasher (R32)	1989 - 1990	Main fuse/relay panel *see also* Turn signal flasher
Emergency flasher switch	All	Center console
Engine compartment fan		*see* Heater blower
Engine compartment fan relay		*see* Heater blower relay
Engine control module (ECM)		*see* DME control unit
Engine speed sensor		*see* Reference/speed sensor
Engine temperature sensor		*see* Cylinder head temperature sensor
Evaporative control valve	C2/C4	Top of engine

Component	Model	Location
Exterior temperature sensor	All	Left mirror
Extra air slide control	Turbo	On engine
EZ69 control unit		*see* Ignition control unit
Flasher relay		*see* Emergency flasher *see also* Turn signal flasher
Foglight relay, front (R31)	All	Main fuse/relay panel
Foglight switch, front	All	Center of dash
Foglight/back-up light relay, rear (R01)	All	Main fuse/relay panel
Frequency transformer (FCU) relay (R24/R52)	All	Main fuse/relay panel
Fresh air blower	All	*see* Windshield defroster blower
Fuel injectors	All	Right and left sides of engine
Fuel level gauge	All	Instrument cluster
Fuel level sender	All	Top of fuel tank in luggage compartment
Fuel pump	C2/C4	Front suspension subframe
Fuel pump relay (R41)	C2/C4	Main fuse/relay panel
Fuel pump relay (R61)	Turbo	Main fuse/relay panel
Fuel pump, front	Turbo	Front suspension subframe
Fuel pump, rear	Turbo	Right rear engine compartment
Fuse/relay panel, front	All	Luggage compartment, right rear
Fuse/relay panel, rear	All	Engine compartment, left
Gear position switch	Tiptronic	On transmission
Generator		*see* Alternator
Glove compartment light	All	In dash, above glove compartment door
Gong relay	All	Left side steering column
Hall sender	C2/C4	In ignition distributor
Hazard warning switch		*see* Emergency flasher switch
Headlight dimmer switch	All	Left side steering column
Headlight switch	All	left side of dash next to ignition switch
Headlight washer pump	All	Washer fluid reservoir in left wheel housing
Headlight washer relay (R43)	All	Main fuse/relay panel
Headlight washer switch	All	Windshield wiper switch
Heater blower relay, rear	All	Engine compartment fuse/relay panel
Heater blower resistor	C2/C4	In engine compartment
Heater blower resistor, rear, left/right	Turbo	In left/right rear wheel housing
Heater blower switch	C2/C4	In dash on right side of steering column

Component	Model	Location
Heater blower, rear	All	In left/right rear wheel housing
Heater control	All	In dash on right side of steering column
High beam indicator light	All	Instrument cluster
Horn contacts	All	Steering wheel
Horn relay (R23)	C2/C4	Main fuse/relay panel
Horns, high and low	All	Right front wheel well
Idle control switch	C2/C4	Left side throttle body
Idle speed control valve	C2/C4	Between intake runners
Idle stabilizer	C2/C4	*see* Idle speed control valve
Ignition coil I/II	C2/C4	Left side engine compartment mounted to inner panel
Ignition control unit	Turbo	Engine compartment fuse/relay panel
Ignition control unit I/II	C2/C4	Left side engine compartment mounted to inner panel
Ignition switch	All	Dashboard, left side of steering column
Inside temperature sensor blower	All	Dashboard, right of steering column
Instrument lights	All	Dashboard gauges
Instrument lights control	All	Luggage compartment at left windshield support
Intensive cleaning fluid pump	Turbo	Luggage compartment right side
Intensive cleaning fluid pump relay (R53)	Turbo	Main fuse/relay panel
Interface electronics (on-board computer)	Turbo	Luggage compartment left rear
Interior light, left, right	All	Above doors
Intermittent wiper control		*see* Windshield wiper intermittent relay (R42)
Intermittent wiper switch		*see* Windshield wiper intermittent switch
Kick-down switch	Tiptronic	By accelerator pedal under pedal cluster trim panel
Knock sensor I	C2/C4	Top of engine cylinders 1 - 3, left side
Knock sensor II	C2/C4	Top of engine cylinders 4 - 6, right side
Lateral acceleration sensor	Tiptronic	In center console
Lateral acceleration sensor (ABS)	C4	In center console
Light switch	All	Dashboard, next to ignition switch
Locking differential valves	C4	Luggage compartment floor right front
Longitudinal acceleration sensor	C4	In center console
Luggage compartment light	All	Luggage compartment lid, right rear

Component	Model	Location
Main fuse/relay panel	All	Right rear luggage compartment
Main/fuel pump relay (R 41)	C2/C4	Main fuse/relay panel
Map alteration switch	C2/C4	Under left seat
MFI + DI control unit	C2/C4	Under left seat
MFI + DI relay (R41)	C2/C4	Main fuse/relay panel
Mirror control switch	All	Interior door panel below vent window
Mirror heating switch	All	*see* Rear defogger switch
Oil cooler blower	All	Behind right headlight
Oil cooler blower relay (R04)	All	Main fuse/relay panel
Oil cooler blower resistor	All	Right front wheel well
Oil cooler thermoswitch	All	Top of oil cooler
Oil level transmitter	All	In oil tank in front of right rear wheel
Oil pressure sending module	All	Right side of crankshaft pulley
Oil pressure sensor switch	All	On engine
Oil pressure switch	All	Top of crankcase on flywheel end
Oil temperature sensor (instruments)	All	Right side of crankshaft pulley
Oil temperature sensor (oil cooler fan)		*see* Oil cooler thermoswitch
Oil temperature sensor cooling fan	All	Right front wheel housing
On-board computer		*see* Central informer
Outside mirror heater	All	Outside mirror glass
Oxygen sensor	All	Front of catalytic converter
Oxygen sensor control unit	Turbo	Under left seat
Parking brake contacts	All	Parking brake handle bracket, rear
Power door locks	All	*see* Central locking
Power window relay (R22)	All	Main fuse/relay panel
Pressure sensor	C2/C4	Under left seat
Pressure warning switch		*see* ABS pressure switch
Pulse transmitter	C2/C4	*see* Windshield wiper intermittent relay (R42)
Radio	All	Dashboard, center
Radio speaker crossover	All	Behind left/right door trim panel
Radio speakers, front	All	Left/right door trim panel
Radio speakers, rear	All	Utility shelf, below rear window
Rear foglight cut-out relay	C2/C4	Left side of engine compartment, behind panel
Rear foglight/back-up lights relay (R01)	All	Main fuse/relay panel
Rear spoiler control unit	1989 - 1990 C2/C4	Under right seat

Component	Model	Location
Rear spoiler control unit	1991 on C2/C4	Under right side dashboard
Rear window defogger	All	In rear window
Rear window defogger and mirror heating switch	All	Above radio
Rear window defogger relay	All	Engine compartment fuse/relay panel
Rear window wiper motor	All	At rear window, under parcel shelf
Rear window wiper relay	All	On rear window wiper motor
Rear window wiper switch	C2/C4	Dashboard, between gauges
Reference/speed sensor	Manual trans.	Left side of clutch housing
Reference/speed sensor	Tiptronic	Right side of bellhousing
Seat adjusting motor	All	Seat bottom
Seat adjusting switches	All	Seat bottom
Seat belt warning light	All	Instrument cluster
Seat heater element, backrest	All	Seat back
Seat heater element, cushion	All	Seat bottom
Seat heater relay	All	Seat bottom
Seat heater switch, left/right	All	Left/right seat bottom, with seat adjusting switches
Selector lever lock control unit	Tiptronic	Main fuse/relay panel
Shift lock control unit	Tiptronic	Main fuse/relay panel
Shift valve resonance flap	C2/C4	Right side of bellhousing (Tiptronic transmission)
Speed sensor		*see* Reference/speed sensor
Speedometer	All	Instrument cluster
Speedometer pick-up	All	Left side transmission final drive
Spoiler microswitches	C2/C4	Engine compartment lid left side
Starter	All	Right side transmission bellhousing
Starter relay (with automatic transmission) (R61)	Tiptronic	Main fuse/relay panel
Stop light switch		*see* Brake light switch
Sunroof motor	All	Inside roof headliner between sunroof and rear window
Sunroof relay (R21)	All	Main fuse/relay panel
Sunroof switch	All	Above ignition switch
Tachometer	All	Center gauge in instrument cluster
Tank venting valve		*see* Evaporative control valve

Component	Model	Location
Temperature sensor, cylinder head		*see* Engine temperature sensor
Terminal 15E relay (R11)	All	Main fuse/relay panel
Terminal X relay (R33)	All	Main fuse/relay panel
Thermo-time switch (cold start valve)	Turbo	On left timing chain housing cover
Thermoswitch relay (catalytic converter) (R44)	All	Main fuse/relay panel
Throttle valve switch(es)	All	Throttle housing
Timing valve	Turbo	On engine
Tiptronic transmission control unit	Tiptronic	Under left seat
Turbo charge indicator light	Turbo	Instrument cluster
Turbo charge indicator switch	Turbo	On engine
Turbo charge pressure sensor	Turbo	On engine
Turbocharger control unit	Turbo	Under left seat
Turn signal flasher	All	In center console
Turn signal switch	All	Left side steering column
V-belt control	All	Rear of engine
Vacuum control valve	Turbo	On engine
Variant configuration plugs	C2/C4	Under left seat
Voltage regulator	All	Mounted to rear of alternator
Volume air flow sensor	C2/C4	Top of engine mounted between intake runners
Warning buzzer	Turbo	In instrument cluster
Window motor	All	Inside door
Window switch	All	Interior door panel
Windshield defroster blower	All	Luggage compartment, rear
Windshield defroster switch	All	A/C-heater control in dash
Windshield washer nozzles, heated	All	Front cowl, right and left sides
Windshield washer pump	All	Luggage compartment, in front of battery
Windshield washer switch	All	*see* Windshield wiper/washer switch
Windshield wiper intermittent relay (R42)	All	Main fuse/relay panel
Windshield wiper intermittent switch	All	Dashboard, between speedometer and clock
Windshield wiper motor	All	Behind speedometer and clock
Windshield wiper pulse transmitter	All	*see* Windshield wiper intermittent relay
Windshield wiper/washer switch	All	Right side steering column

Index

Acknowledgments

Bentley Publishers wishes to thank **Jeff Curtis** of Virginia Beach, Virginia; **Bill Gregory** of Brookfield, Connecticut; **Tom Sharpes** of Rancho Cucamonga, California; and **Adrian Streather** of Waltzenhausen AR, Switzerland, for their generous and insightful technical review of this book. Their expertise has helped make this book a more detailed and accurate technical information source for Porsche 964s.

Selected Books and Repair Information From Bentley Publishers

Engineering

Bosch Fuel Injection and Engine Management
Charles O. Probst, SAE ISBN 978-0-8376-0300-1

Maximum Boost: Designing, Testing, and Installing Turbocharger Systems
Corky Bell ISBN 978-0-8376-0160-1

Race Car Aerodynamics *Joseph Katz*
ISBN 978-0-8376-0142-7

Scientific Design of Exhaust and Intake Systems
Phillip H. Smith & John C. Morrison
ISBN 978-0-8376-0309-4

Audi Repair Manuals

Audi TT Service Manual: 2000-2006, 1.8L Turbo, 3.2 L, including Roadster and Quattro
Bentley Publishers ISBN 978-0-8376-1500-4

Audi A6 (C5 platform) Service Manual: 1998-2004, includes A6, Allroad Quattro, S6, RS6
Bentley Publishers ISBN 978-0-8376-1499-1

BMW Repair Manuals

BMW X5 (E53) Service Manual: 2000-2006
Bentley Publishers ISBN 978-0-8376-1534-9

BMW 3 Series (E46) Service Manual: 1999-2005
Bentley Publishers ISBN 978-0-8376-1277-5

Porsche Literature

Porsche Boxster Service Manual: 1997-2004
Bentley Publishers ISBN 978-0-8376-1333-8

Porsche 911 Carrera Service Manual: 1984-1989
Bentley Publishers ISBN 978-0-8376-0291-2

Porsche 911 SC Service Manual: 1987-1983
Bentley Publishers ISBN 978-0-8376-0290-5

Ferdinand Porsche: Genesis of Genius
Karl Ludvigsen ISBN 978-0-8376-1334-5

Porsche: Excellence Was Expected
Karl Ludvigsen ISBN 978-0-8376-0235-5

Volkswagen Repair Manuals

Volkswagen Jetta Service Manual: 2005-2006
Bentley Publishers ISBN 978-0-8376-1364-2

Volkswagen Jetta, Golf, GTI Service Manual: 1999-2005 *Bentley Publishers*
ISBN 978-0-8376-1251-5

Volkswagen Passat Service Manual: 1998-2005
Bentley Publishers ISBN 978-0-8376-1483-0

Motorsports

Alex Zanardi: My Sweetest Victory
Alex Zanardi with Gianluca Gasparini
ISBN 978-0-8376-1249-2

Driving Forces *Peter Stevenson*
ISBN 978-0-8376-0217-2

Going Faster! Mastering the Art of Race Driving
Carl Lopez ISBN 978-0-8376-0226-4

Sports Car and Competition Driving
Paul Frére ISBN 978-0-8376-0202-8

Automotive Reference

Bentley Publishers has published service manuals and automobile books since 1950. For more information, please contact Bentley Publishers at 1734 Massachusetts Avenue, Cambridge, MA 02138, visit our web site at **www.BentleyPublishers.com** or call 1-800-423-4595 for a free copy of our complete catalog.

eBahn.com®